GW01112354

THE LETTERS TO THE SEVEN CHURCHES OF ASIA

The Letters to the Seven Churches of Asia

W. L. Bedwell

THE CHRISTADELPHIAN
404 SHAFTMOOR LANE
BIRMINGHAM B28 8SZ
ENGLAND
1988

First published 1988

ISBN 0 85189 121 7

Reproduced from copy supplied.
Printed and bound in Great Britain
by Billing and Sons Limited
Worcester

PREFACE

THE student of the Book of Revelation, in his understandable desire to move into the great visions of the Apocalypse, may be inclined to pass over the first three chapters—or to give them the briefest of consideration. It is not surprising, then, if in some expositions of Revelation, less attention has been given to these Letters.

This book is an attempt to give the Seven Letters to the Ecclesias of Asia the detailed treatment which they deserve. The reader will soon discover how rich in exhortation are these opening chapters of the book; but also how essential they are in setting the scene for the Apocalypse as a whole.

The chapters began as articles in *The Christadelphian* magazine, between November 1984 and April 1986, and are republished here in more permanent form and commended to the Brotherhood.

Most of the Scripture quotations in this book are from the Revised Standard Version.

Contents

1. INTRODUCTION 1
2. SEVEN CHURCHES, SEVEN ANGELS,
   SEVEN STARS 12
3. THE LETTER TO EPHESUS 17
4. THE LETTER TO SMYRNA 35
5. THE LETTER TO PERGAMOS 47
6. THE LETTER TO THYATIRA 65
7. THE LETTER TO SARDIS 82
8. THE LETTER TO PHILADELPHIA 93
9. THE LETTER TO LAODICEA 104
10. TO HIM WHO CONQUERS 121

1

INTRODUCTION

BEFORE we can apply the messages in these letters to ourselves, we must know something of the world in which the recipients lived and the meaning the letters had for them. The title Asia refers to the Roman province of Asia and not to the continent of Asia. This province comprised the western part of Asia Minor and is now part of Turkey.

A Jewish Population

Alexander the Great had planted Greek cities and Greek influence over a wide area and this influence survived his death in 323 B.C. especially in Asia Minor. Alexander's vast domain was divided among his generals and finally developed into three great empires. Asia Minor formed part of what became known as the Seleucid empire. There was a considerable Jewish element in this empire. Deportations from Palestine to the Euphrates districts by the Assyrians, Chaldeans and to a lesser extent, Persians led to a substantial Jewish population in these districts. About 200 B.C. Antiochus the Great sent 2000 Jewish families from Babylonia to cities in Asia Minor. Privileges were granted to those who migrated and the dissemination of Jews in this area would also be encouraged by opportunities for trade which followed the Greek conquest.

At about the time of Alexander's death, Rome began to extend her influence over the rest of Italy and within a century had broken the power of Carthage in North Africa. The next two centuries saw a spectacular increase in the power of Rome and she absorbed the empires of Alexander's successors. Roman power was then acknowledged in a series of provinces, protectorates and client states which ringed the Mediterranean and made this a Roman sea.

THE LETTERS TO THE SEVEN CHURCHES OF ASIA

Travel in the Mediterranean area during the first century A.D. was safer and easier than at any subsequent time until the late 19th century. The Mediterranean was a life-line of the empire, carrying food to Rome. The ship of Alexandria on which Paul travelled to Rome would have a cargo of grain for the capital. The sea lanes were closed by the weather for at least four months of the year.

The problem of administering this vast area led to the emergence of strong men in Rome. After a series of power struggles, Octavian emerged as the undisputed leader and was given the title Augustus. The emperor organised the provinces and settled their administration. He set up a permanent standing army and the power of Rome after the establishment of the empire was based on this army. Augustus placed the legions where danger was most likely but it was essential to be able to move troops from place to place as quickly as possible to meet new dangers.

A Vast Road System

Rome therefore became the centre of a vast system of roads (see Maps 1 and 2) built to connect the capital with the provinces of the empire with the minimum connection between the subject countries so that each looked to Rome as the centre and regarded the others as rivals for the favour of Rome. However, as we shall see, the roads connecting the provinces in Asia Minor were fairly well developed because in many cases the roads that led to Rome also connected the various provinces with one another. They were built primarily for military purposes but were also used for commerce. It was along some of these roads that Paul travelled. The nodal points in the system of Roman roads were the great cities of the empire, such as Alexandria, Antioch in Syria, Corinth and Ephesus. Roman police maintained law and order along these roads although bandits were not entirely eliminated. The remarkable network of Roman roads was even more important to the empire than the sea lanes and provided facilities for land travel unsurpassed until railways were built, although some roads which crossed mountains were closed during the winter.

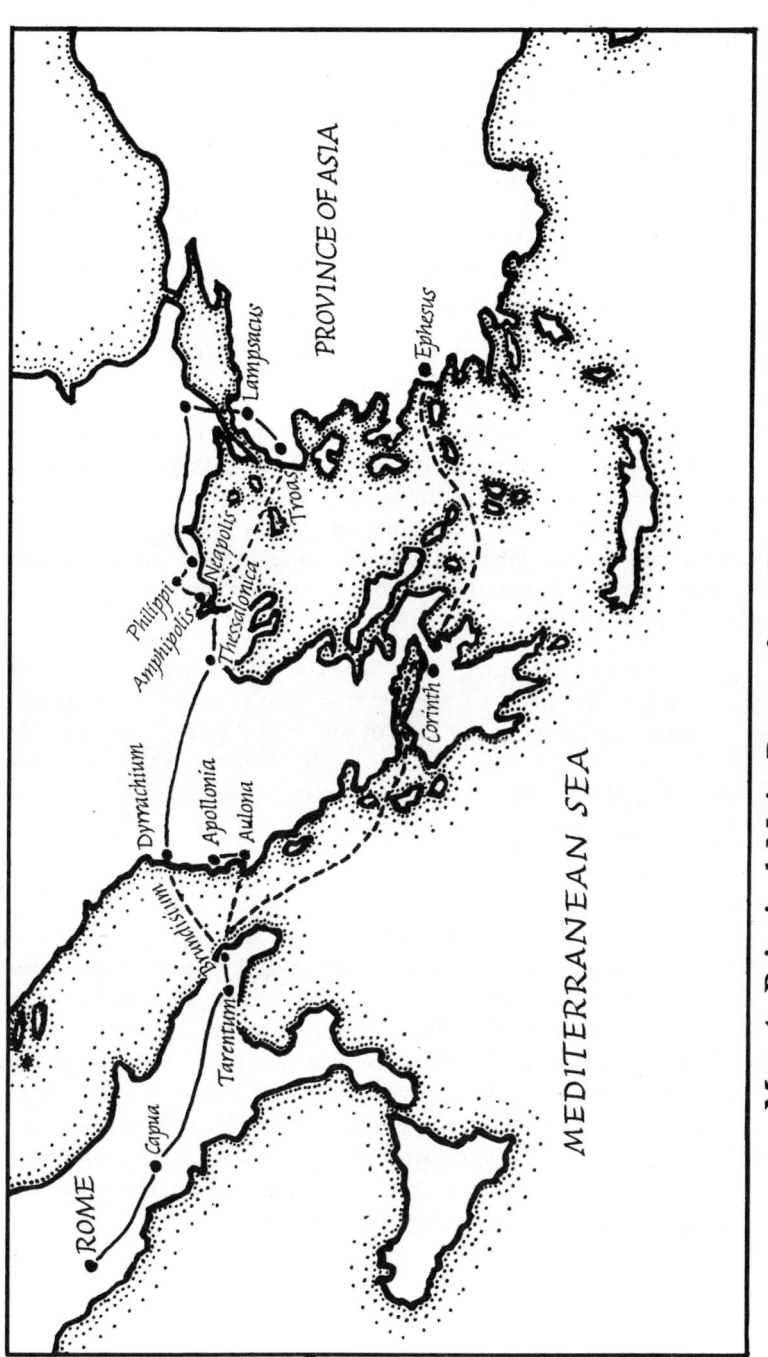

Map 1: Principal Main Routes from Rome to Asia Minor

THE LETTERS TO THE SEVEN CHURCHES OF ASIA

We must now look at the geography of Asia Minor. The mass of Asia Minor is a high plateau cut by four river valleys which form narrow clefts in the plateau, and separated by mountain chains which stretch out to the west like fingers (Ramsay). The roads connecting Rome with Mesopotamia, Syria and Palestine must necessarily follow the lines of these four valleys. Near the mouth of each of them stood a Greek city in which the importance of the valley was centred.

The four valleys, from north to south, are those of:

(1) The river **Caikos**, with the city of Pergamum about 15 miles from the sea and 3 miles north of the river, which was navigable to this point for the small ancient ships. Pergamum was a great and famous city which at the time John wrote was capital of the province. Built on a high conical hill which dominated the broad and fertile valley, Pergamum handled much of the produce of the hinterland but it was never a centre of international commerce like Ephesus or Smyrna.

(2) The river **Hermus**, with the city of Smyrna which was situated at the head of and on the south side of a deep and sheltered gulf which ran about 30 miles inland. It was the emporium for the trade of the fertile Hermus valley and the terminus of an older route to the interior. Smyrna had become one of the greatest and wealthiest cities of Asia.

(3) The river **Cayster**, with Ephesus on its southern bank. The city had an excellent harbour and was within three miles of the sea. The river was then navigable as far up as the city and measures were taken to prevent silt brought down by the river from choking the waterway to the sea. Despite keen competition Ephesus had established itself in the first century A.D. as the main sea terminal for traffic to the east although it did not become the official capital of the province until the second century A.D. It was one of the three great cities of the East Mediterranean lands, the other two being Antioch in Syria and Alexandria. The population of Ephesus at the time John wrote was probably around a third of a million people.

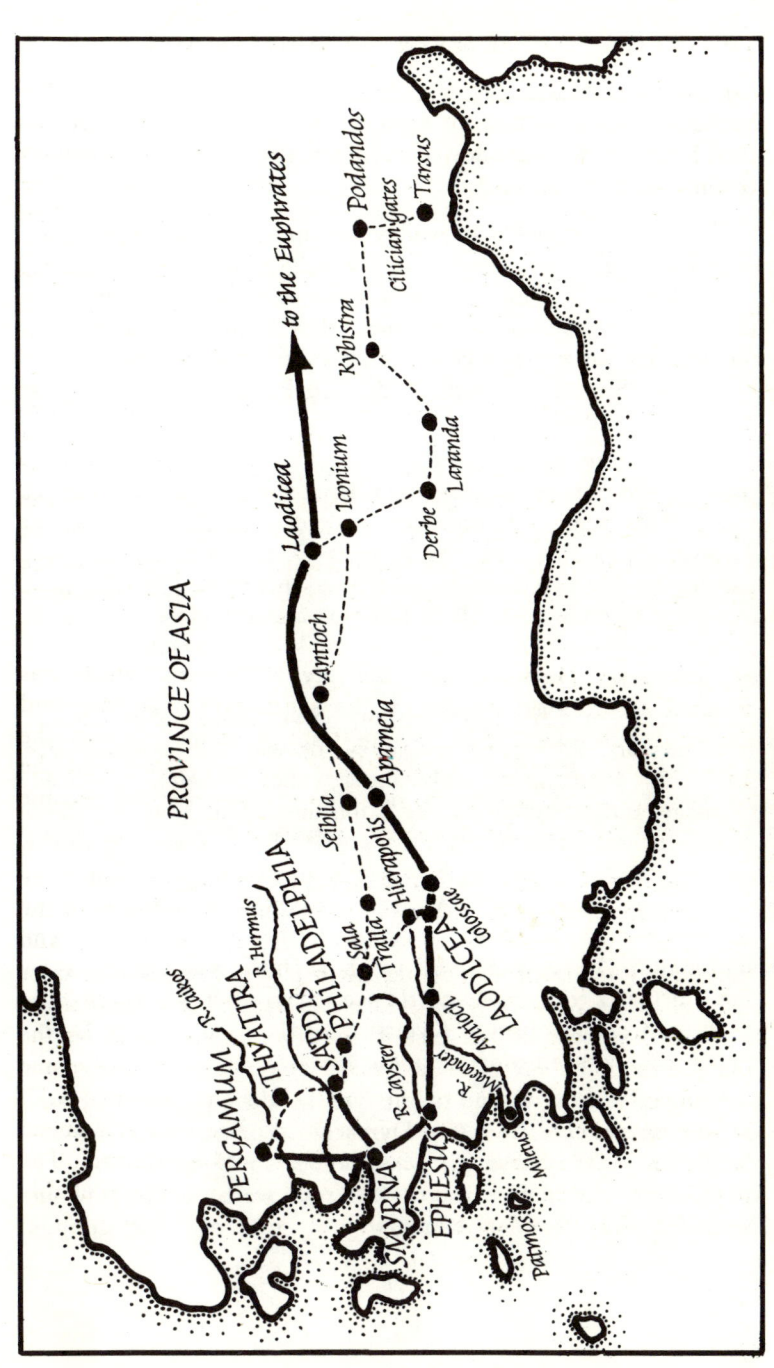

Map 2: Asia Minor—Road System to the East through the Valleys

THE LETTERS TO THE SEVEN CHURCHES OF ASIA

(4) The river **Maeander**, with Miletus. Initially Miletus, with a harbour superior to that for Ephesus, had the advantage over its rival but the river was allowed to silt up, thus diminishing the excellence of the harbour.

The terrain of the Caikos valley was difficult. There was an old overland route from Pergamum which joined the road from Smyrna at Sardis, but it was unsuitable as a main road for heavy traffic. The terrain of the Hermus valley from Smyrna was also too difficult for a major commercial route although there was a road from Smyrna through Sardis and Philadelphia to the east and to the hinterland.

A road from Ephesus through the Cayster valley joined the road from Smyrna, but was too difficult for a major commercial route. This road did, however, provide the shortest route to Antioch in Pisidia and was therefore often preferred by foot passengers. Paul seems to have followed this route when journeying from Pisidian Antioch to Ephesus and therefore did not go through Colossae, so that he was not known personally to the ecclesia there.

The main road from Pergamum, Smyrna and Ephesus to the east therefore did not use the valleys on which these cities were sited, but went up the Maeander valley through Laodicea, Colossae and Apameia to the Euphrates. This road has been described as a great artery through which the life-blood of the empire mainly flowed and the cities on this route grew steadily in importance. Travellers for Antioch in Syria, Palestine and Egypt left the main road at a second city also called Laodicea and went via Iconium, Derbe and Kybistra, through the pass known as the Cilician Gates to Tarsus and thence to Syria. It was possible to go direct from Iconium to Kybistra but the road through Derbe seems to have been more popular.

A traveller from Rome to the east would go down to Brundisium, and thence by sea to Dyrrachium or Aulona and along the Egnatian Way through Thessalonica to Neapolis, the port of Philippi. Alternative routes to Troas were possible beyond Neapolis. The traveller then had the choice of going through

INTRODUCTION

Pergamum by the older shorter route to the east via Thyatira, Sardis and Philadelphia or on the longer main road through Pergamum, Smyrna and Ephesus to Laodicea. An alternative route from Rome was by sea from the port of Brundisium to the Isthmus of Corinth, across this narrow strip of land, and by sea again from Corinth to Ephesus. Imperial despatches for most of the year went by the overland route through Macedonia and Greece. It was shorter than the alternative sea route and being fully maintained throughout the year, it was the main route for administrative purposes.

We can now appreciate the importance of Asia Minor, and in particular Ephesus, to the Roman trade with the Euphrates. The seven ecclesias were situated in large towns in one of the most prosperous, populous and intellectually active of the Roman provinces. Apart from the three ports, Thyatira, Sardis and Philadelphia were situated on the older overland route from Pergamum and Smyrna to the east, to which Laodicea had easy access. The order in which the letters appear in Revelation 2 and 3 is the order in which a messenger from Patmos and landing at Ephesus would reach the seven cities.

In this area, oriental, Greek, Jewish and Roman religions and cultures met. We may take Ephesus as typical of the region. It stood midway between two continents, being on the one hand the gateway to Asia and on the other hand the rendezvous of multitudes of Eastern pilgrims coming to worship at the temple of Diana. Traversed by the great imperial highway, it had all nationalities meeting and mingling in its streets. In Ephesus a noble freedom of thought and a vulgar superstition lived side by side (Ramsay, *Dictionary of the Apostolic Church,* Vol. 1, p. 350).

The vulgar superstition was centred in the worship of Diana, or, more properly, Artemis (R.S.V.), a goddess with little in common with the chaste virgin huntress, goddess of Greek mythology. Worshipped in Ephesus long before the Greeks came, Artemis represented the reproductive powers of the human race and of animals. The Phoenician Astarte or Ashteroth, mentioned in the Old Testament, the Phrygian Cybele etc., are probably all different names under which the goddess was worshipped.

THE LETTERS TO THE SEVEN CHURCHES OF ASIA

"Great is Diana..."

The upper part of statues of the body of the goddess were covered with rows of breasts to symbolise her function as nourishing all life. Her worship was accompanied by ceremonial prostitution by temple-slaves of both sexes who were at the service of the worshippers. The proximity of the temple of the goddess, one of the greatest and most famous architectural works of the ancient world, gave it immense power in the city. Ephesus owed its preeminence in Asia in part to this temple and boasted of the title of "warden of the temple of Artemis" (cf. Acts 19:35, R.V. and R.S.V.).

The festivals of the goddess were thronged by pilgrims from Asia and contributed greatly to the wealth of the city. In addition to the priests and priestesses who enjoyed the rich revenue of her temple, many trades were mainly dependent on the pilgrims who required food, entertainment, sacrifices, offerings and images to take away with them. These vested interests were able to rouse the mob to demonstrate for the goddess (Acts 19).

With the spread of the Graeco-Roman civilisation there was a conflict between the native primitive oriental culture of the country and the new European ideas. "All who got any education learned the Greek language, adopted Greek manners, ... called themselves, their children and their gods by Greek names, and affected to identify their religion with that of Greece and Rome. All this class of persons despised the native language and the native ways ..." (Ramsay, *The Church in the Roman Empire*, pp. 41-42).

The Imperial Government recognised more fully than any administration before or for centuries afterward, the need to maintain a tolerable standard of comfort among the poorer classes of citizens. But while it showed great zeal as regards their physical comfort by feeding and amusing them, it did nothing to provide a satisfying religion (*The Church in the Roman Empire*, pp. 359-360). Greek philosophy had little influence on life except to produce "disbelief in current religions and contempt for the most vulgar kinds of superstition ... people tolerated the duties as traditional

INTRODUCTION

ceremonial, and enjoyed the festivals merely as fine shows''. "The best mind of the age was wistfully awaiting a new order of things" (Ramsay, *Hastings Dictionary of the Bible*, Vol. 5, pp. 154-5; *Dictionary of the Apostolic Church*, Vol. 1, p. 350). A new and morally revolutionary way, which had a direct bearing on belief and manner of life, arrived with Christianity (Acts 19).

"Those who feared God"

A third element in the mixture of ideas was provided by the Jewish religion. The Jews of Asia were not absorbed by the surrounding pagan religions but practised strict Judaism, building synagogues in which to worship. They seem to have conducted successful propaganda among the surrounding pagans who were attracted by their exemplary family life and by the morality of their religion and strict Sabbath observance. Greek became the mother tongue of the Jews (except in Babylonia) and the Old Testament was translated into Greek for their use. This also helped to make their religion better understood by their Greek-speaking neighbours, large numbers of whom accepted circumcision and became proselytes. In addition, large numbers of non-Jews attended synagogues without actually becoming proselytes —"those who feared God" (Acts 13:16,26).

Wherever Jews lived in any number, they organised themselves into societies to maintain their uniqueness, safeguard their interests and practise their worship. When the Jews were present in a city merely as resident aliens, it was easy for them to retain and practise their religion, but in some cities, for example those founded by the Seleucid kings, the Jews were actually citizens. Jews and other citizens in such a city were grouped in bodies known by the Greeks as tribes. Each tribe was united by a religious bond, the members met in worship of a common deity or deities and their unity lay in their participation in the same religion. Jews could therefore practise their religion as one of these tribes in private association without any bond of pagan religion. But there was a difficulty. The entire body of citizens were knit together by a general acceptance of the gods worshipped in the city. Clearly, the Jews stood apart from this city cultus, abhorring and despising it. The Seleucid kings permitted Jews to disregard the common city cultus and absolved them from the ordinary laws and regulations of the city if these conflicted with the Jewish religion. This was a constant source of friction between Jews and their fellow-citizens who took the view that if Jews desired to be citizens, they must honour the gods of the city. A Jew who sought to join another tribe for advantages in trade etc. would have had to participate in the religion of that tribe and worship its gods, thus denying his own God.

A Lawful Religion

The Romans confirmed the privileges granted by the Seleucid kings and permitted the free exercise of the Jewish religion. Julius Caesar and Augustus in particular maintained and enlarged the privileges of the Jews. These comprised the right of administering their own funds including the collection and transmission of the dues paid to the temple in Jerusalem, jurisdiction over their own members and freedom from military service. By and large this attitude was maintained by later emperors. The Romans regarded Judaism as a "lawful religion" and, when emperor worship became the norm, Jews were exempted from this. Christianity in its early years was regarded as an offshoot of the Jewish religion and similarly exempted from the cult of the Emperor. Later in the first century, before John wrote, this ceased and the Christian who believed Jesus is Lord could not offer incense to an emperor and call him Lord, and so he risked death.

In Ephesus, still using this as a typical example, there were several powers which were brought into contact or conflict in the first two centuries A.D. Among these were the hierarchy of the temple of Artemis, the government of the city and Christianity. Initially, as Acts 19 states, the government of the city sided with the Christians but, towards the end of the first century the persecution of the Christians under Domitian and the realisation that the growing power of Christianity would destroy the worship of Artemis led all who were not Christians to combine in an attempt to preserve the existing order in the city.

INTRODUCTION

Lessons for Today

We close this introduction by drawing attention to similarities between the first century and our own age. Professor Martin, in a book published in 1968, stated that the age in which the New Testament was written was a materialistic age. The inhabitants of the cities were interested, first and foremost, in making money and enjoying the comforts and luxuries it provided. One reason for this materialism was the failure of the old Graeco-Roman religion but the basic cause was the view of the cosmos provided by Greek science. He wrote: "The new scientific world-view, which placed emphasis on transcendence, universal law and cosmic order, pushed religion into a phase of pessimism and despair. Scientists had given an important place to the stars and planets in their systems. Astrologers made capital of this by teaching that everything in this world—including the lot of humanity—was determined by astral powers indifferent to the individual . . . and the particular constellation or conjunction of the stars or planets under which a person was born was of decisive importance—determined 'the entire course of our lives, and . . . nothing can enable us to escape' " (*New Testament Foundations*, 2, pp. 31-32). And, as we have seen, there was sexual licence among sections of the population.

A multiracial, materialistic society in which there was sexual licence, a conflict of science and religion and a concern with astrology. We could be describing our own age! We may find, therefore, these seven letters very relevant to our own situation, because believers then and now can be influenced more than they realise by the spirit of the age in which they live.

2

SEVEN CHURCHES, SEVEN ANGELS, SEVEN STARS

EACH of the letters contains the words *"He that hath an ear, let him hear what the Spirit saith unto the churches"*, words similar to those often used by Jesus in the Gospels. The letters, although sent to individual ecclesias, were not meant solely for them. The number seven is used by John much more frequently than any other number. There were seven golden candlesticks, seven lamps of fire before the throne, seven seals, seven trumpets, seven thunders. Seven was the number of completion and the seven ecclesias represented the whole brotherhood. There were at that time ecclesias in Asia other than those named by John. These seven were selected to show the problems the brotherhood then faced and their reactions to them. Other ecclesias might not find themselves in identical circumstances to any one of these ecclesias but, looking at the letters as a whole, they could see themselves in that mirror in one characteristic or another of the seven ecclesias, and assess their standing in the Lord's sight. This is true not only of that generation but of all succeeding ones until the Lord comes. Here for us also are the various conditions in which ecclesias today can be found. We must look into this mirror, disguising nothing but seeing in it our individual selves and ecclesias, and note the warnings and danger signals.

Conflict with the Authorities

When John wrote, the brotherhood was moving into conflict with the Roman Government. Rome required its subjects, with few exceptions, to worship the emperor. Rome failed to understand why Christians, unlike their pagan neighbours, would not accept the emperor as one of the gods and offer a pinch of incense

SEVEN CHURCHES, SEVEN ANGELS, SEVEN STARS

on his altar. Christians, believing that Jesus alone is Lord, refused to give this title to the earthly ruler. They could not compromise and Rome, therefore, attempted to break their allegiance to Christ by persecution and death. The province of Asia was the centre of the imperial religion, where the first temples to the emperor had been built and where his worship was most fully developed. The problem thus came to a head in Asia and John prepared the ecclesias for their test of faith.

The society in which modern believers live is largely pagan and presents problems to us just as it did to the early brotherhood. Rome persecuted the early Christians not for their beliefs as such but for their refusal to acknowledge the supremacy of the State. We may encounter this problem in these closing days of Gentile times. We do not know in detail what the future holds for us. We have entered the nuclear age with the possibility of a nuclear holocaust so terrible as to be beyond our conception. In this nuclear age are also problems of adequate food for the earth's population, energy supply, pollution etc. These are so pressing and difficult to solve that some around us realise that we are coming to the end of an age.

The Lord warned us that before his return there will be distress on earth with no way out, *"men fainting with fear and with foreboding of what is coming on the world"* (Luke 21:26, R.S.V.). For the sake of the elect, those days will be shortened, otherwise none would be saved. We may then encounter problems with the authorities for which our experience in recent years has left us ill-prepared. The letters which spoke to the first century brotherhood in its difficult and dangerous position will have a message for us in our modern world as it becomes increasingly difficult and dangerous to us.

The Lord Exalted

We come now to the author of these letters as presented to us in Revelation 1. John saw the Lord in the midst of seven golden lampstands and described him as a person of surpassing power and majesty to whom divine attributes had been given. The beloved disciple had been closest to Jesus in his life on earth and had reclined in his bosom at the Last Supper (John 13:23, R.V.) but now in awe at this sublime manifestation of the risen Lord fell at his feet as one dead. John tells us that *"he laid his right hand—the symbol of power—upon me, saying, 'Fear not, I am the first and the last, and the living one. I died, and behold, I am alive for evermore, and I have the keys of Death and Hades' "* (Revelation 1:17-18). The words and actions are characteristic of the Jesus described in the Gospels (e.g. Matthew 14:27,31; Mark 6:50; Luke 24:37-39).

John had been one of the eyewitnesses of the Lord's majesty at the transfiguration. Then also he, Peter and James, *"fell on their faces and were filled with awe. But Jesus came and touched them, saying 'Rise and have no fear' "* (Matthew 17:6-7). The words and action of the risen Lord would remind John of this earlier occasion and reassure him that the Lord he saw in glory was the one he had known so well. But even as Jesus dispelled John's fear, he emphasised his own status by immediately applying to himself a title of God: *"I am the first and I am the last"* (cf. Isaiah 44:6 and 48:12). He added *"and the living one"*, words which would recall the phrase *"the living God"* so often used in the Old Testament (e.g. Psalm 42:2). In Jesus now dwelt all the fulness of the Godhead bodily (Colossians 2:9). All authority in heaven and on earth, God's authority, had been given to the Lord (Matthew 28:18), who now upholds all things by the word of his power (Hebrews 1:3) and is praised in the New Testament in words used in the Old Testament of God himself (Philippians 2:10; Isaiah 45:23).

The Lord in Majesty

The other disciples also had to bring their conception of Jesus into line with the majesty of the risen Lord. Just before the transfiguration, Peter had felt able to remonstrate with Jesus almost as with an equal, telling him that his death at Jerusalem, of which the Lord had just spoken, would never happen (Matthew 16:22). Six weeks after the resurrection, Peter told Jews at Pentecost that *"God hath made him both Lord and Christ, this Jesus whom ye crucified"* (Acts 2:36). And later he described Jesus to Cornelius as *"Lord of all"* (Acts 10:36). This conception of the greatness of the risen Lord was added to their memory of him as a man of deep compassion and understanding.

Modern disciples can have an inadequate conception of the majesty of their risen Lord. We thank God that he was made like his brethren in every respect, able therefore to sympathise with their weaknesses and not ashamed to call them brethren. Nevertheless we must always remember the highly exalted position Jesus now occupies and honour the Son even as we honour the Father (John 5:23). Let us listen in deep reverence to what this Lord has to say to us in the letters.

The brotherhood when John wrote was a relatively small community, persecuted by powerful foes. The glory and power of the risen Lord are emphasised to encourage them and there are many indications in this chapter of the care of this majestic one for his people. In verse 5 John speaks of Jesus as *"him who loves us"* (not *"loved"* as in the Authorised Version). The love of Jesus for his people was not shown once for all in his sacrifice but continues throughout our lives.

The Lord in the Midst

The seven golden lampstands represent the seven ecclesias. The figure is reminiscent of the seven-branched lampstand of the Old Testament (Exodus 25; Zechariah 4) but here the lampstands are separate. The ecclesias were individually responsible for their actions but Jesus was in their midst and they were united by him. The same symbolism is seen in the seven stars, the angels, who are all held in the Lord's right hand. The phrase *"in the midst"* is often used in the Old Testament to encourage God's people. *"God is in the midst of her, she shall not be moved"* (Psalm 46:5; cf. Isaiah 12:6; Zephaniah 3:15; Zechariah 2:10). Here, in the midst of the ecclesias, is the Lord with power far greater than that of their adversaries and they will not be moved. He cares for them and watches over them, even although they may have to suffer and die for his name, but— *"I died, and behold I am alive for evermore, and I have the keys of Death and Hades."* If they died, their Lord was able to release them from death and the grave. Therefore, the Lord said to John, because of what you have seen and heard, my

THE LETTERS TO THE SEVEN CHURCHES OF ASIA

power, my care for the ecclesias, my ability to save from death, write to the seven churches to show them their condition in my sight and tell them of events to come.

The same Lord is in the midst of the ecclesias today to act as their bond of union, to care for and watch over them and ultimately to redeem them from death. The vision of Revelation can be, should be a source of strength and comfort to them as it was to the ecclesias 1900 years ago.

We shall see later that a title of Jesus, appropriate to the circumstances in each ecclesia, is used to introduce the letters and that these can be used to warn as well as to comfort. It is unnecessary here to consider in detail who the angel of the ecclesia was. Suffice it to say that, for example, the elders in Ephesus (appointed under the guidance of the Spirit) who were summoned to meet Paul at Miletus were in all probability the angel of the ecclesia. Each letter is addressed to the angel but intended for the ecclesia, the angel is identified with the ecclesia and no distinction is made between them when praise or blame is apportioned. In modern terms, the letter for the ecclesia would first go to the Arranging Brethren through the recording brother (although these "elders" are elected and not appointed under the direct guidance of the Spirit). The spiritual condition of an ecclesia and its leaders is usually very similar. Enthusiastic elders will beget an enthusiastic ecclesia and lackadaisical elders a lifeless community. There is therefore a great responsibility on ecclesial leaders to set the highest possible spiritual tone.

3

THE LETTER TO EPHESUS

IT IS unnecessary to add to what was said about the city itself in the introductory chapter but some consideration of the beginning of the ecclesia in Ephesus will help our understanding of the letter the Lord later sent to it. Paul paid a brief visit to Ephesus with Priscilla and Aquila (Acts 18) whom he left in Ephesus, where they met and converted Apollos. Paul later returned to Ephesus (Acts 19), spending more than two years there in such active service that Luke records that "all the residents of Asia heard the word of the Lord, both Jews and Greeks" (v. 10). Paul had recognised the importance of this city in the dissemination of the Gospel in the province of Asia, which seems to have been evangelised, at least in part, by men trained by Paul rather than by the apostle himself. Paul was, therefore, unknown in person to some at least of the ecclesias in Asia (e.g. Colossae). The seven ecclesias to whom the Lord wrote could well have been founded at this time. Later in the first century the apostle John settled in Ephesus, from whence he had been exiled to Patmos.

Statements of Faith

Paul had committed to the Asian converts, as to all believers, a form, a standard of doctrine. The word doctrine in the New Testament is a translation of two Greek words (*didaskalia* and *didachē*), each meaning "teaching". These words have a wider meaning than the term doctrine as we use it and refer not only to the things most surely believed among us (Luke 1) but also to the changed manner of life which must result from these beliefs. Thus Paul lists moral evils as contrary to sound doctrine (1 Timothy 1:9-10). There is reason to believe that very early in the life of the Church, the apostles prepared statements covering both of these aspects. Passages in the New Testament show constructions which seem to have resulted from the translation of such statements from the apostles' mother tongue into Greek. Paul wrote to the Romans that they had become obedient to that form or pattern of teaching to which they were committed. It was obviously wrong for Christians to depart from this pattern but Paul had to warn the elders of Ephesus that *"from among your own selves will men arise speaking perverse things, to draw away the disciples after them. Therefore be alert"* (Acts 20:30-31). *"Take heed to yourselves and to all the flock, in which the Holy Spirit has made you guardians, to feed the church of the Lord"* (v. 28).

Guarding the Deposit

Paul had urged Timothy to stay in Ephesus that he might *"charge certain persons not to teach any different doctrine nor to occupy themselves with myths or endless genealogies"* (1 Timothy 1:3-4). Timothy is also warned that *"in later times some will depart from the faith"* (1 Timothy 4:1), *"will not endure sound teaching . . . and wander into myths"* (2 Timothy 4:3-4). Timothy was, therefore, instructed to guard the deposit (1 Timothy 6:20; 2 Timothy 1:14), *"the pattern of sound words which you have heard from me"* (2 Timothy 1:13) so that he could hand this on inviolate. Coupled with this, Paul exhorted Timothy to hard work—the word means "labour to weariness" (2 Timothy 2:6)—so that Timothy might be *"a workman who has no need to be ashamed"* (2 Timothy 2:15). *"Endure suffering, do the work of an evangelist"* (2 Timothy 4:5). *"Take your share of suffering (R.V. hardship)"* (2 Timothy 2:3).

With this background, we come to the letter itself. *"To the angel of the church in Ephesus write: 'The words of him who holds the seven stars in his right hand and who walks among the seven golden lampstands'."*

The Lord's use of descriptive aspects of himself from Revelation 1 not only introduces this first letter but seems also to introduce the letters as a whole since they describe his relation to all the ecclesias and not merely one. But changes are made from Revelation 1 to encourage them. In that chapter the Lord *has* the seven stars in his right hand but a much stronger word is used in the letter. He *holds* them, or better, firmly grasps them and

THE LETTER TO EPHESUS

using his own words, *"no one shall snatch them out of my hand"* (John 10:28). They are completely in his power, under his almighty protection. Again, in Revelation 1, the Lord was in the midst of the lampstands but in the letter he is walking among them. The priest in the tabernacle or temple, trimming the lamps in the seven-branched golden lampstand and maintaining their oil supply, would appear to an onlooker to be moving among the seven branches. So Jesus walked among the seven lampstands, unceasingly active on their behalf, to enable them to shine as lights in the world. The Lord, walking in the midst of the ecclesias, knew at first hand what was happening to them. He was fully cognisant of their difficulties and problems, their successes and failures.

This could be a warning as well as a comfort. Ecclesias could not hide anything from the Lord nor could any save them if he relinquished his hold on them. The same Lord walks in the modern brotherhood, fully aware of our temptations and problems, successes and failures. We may present a good face to our brethren and sisters, or to other ecclesias but the Lord sees us as we really are. It is for us to look at ourselves through our Lord's eyes and adjust our manner of life accordingly.

"I know your works, your toil and your patient endurance, and how you cannot bear evil men but have tested those who call themselves apostles but are not, and found them to be false. I know you are enduring patiently and bearing up for my name's sake, and you have not grown weary." Here, as in all the letters, Jesus first acknowledged whatever good he found in the ecclesias. Sometimes his people tend to forget his example and concentrate on the faults and failings of fellow disciples.

Labour unto Weariness

The works at Ephesus consisted of toil, patient endurance and resistance to false teaching. Endurance in an ecclesia is not always combined with active exertion but here it was. The word *kopos* translated "toil" (A.V. "labour") means labour to weariness. It refers to the lassitude or weariness which follows when persons strain their powers to the uttermost—and yet (v. 3) they had not grown weary. There is a play on words here. They had toiled until they were weary but they had never wearied of their toil. You remember that the Lord, wearied (same Greek word) with his journey, sat down on Jacob's well but was not weary of his toil for he immediately resumed it when the woman of Samaria appeared.

The word rendered "patient endurance" (*hupomonē*) is always used in the New Testament of patience with regard to things. Thus James, using the same Greek word, writes of the "patience" (A.V.), "steadfastness" (R.S.V.), "endurance" (R.V.m.) of Job. The word denotes active perseverance as well as endurance, a conquering fortitude which the Christian calls on to overcome obstacles, persecutions, sufferings and temptations. He does not lose heart or courage as he meets them; they do not deflect him from the Truth nor affect his loyalty to his Lord. Another word (*makrothumia*) is used of patience in respect of persons, for example, the longsuffering of God to men. We shall return to this when considering verse 4.

Refusing the Evil

They were intolerant of evil men, those who named the name of Christ but would not depart from evil. They had tested and rejected false apostles (cf. 2 Corinthians 11:13; 1 John 4:1; 2 John 10). These had appeared in Paul's lifetime (2 Corinthians 11:13) and had probably multiplied in the intervening years. They claimed apostolic authority for teaching contrary to the "deposit" given the early Christians. Some may have been trying to adapt Christianity to current thought, such as the Gnostic beliefs which John condemned in his first epistle and which would have destroyed Christian morality. Again there is a play on words. They could not bear evil men but they could and did bear reproaches for the name of Christ.

What a eulogy! Persistent in toil, unwearying in service, maintaining purity of life and doctrine, and enduring all the untoward events that happened to them. They had taken to heart Paul's instructions to Timothy at which we looked. The qualities Paul inculcated were here in Ephesus, hard work, endurance, correct

THE LETTER TO EPHESUS

doctrine—and yet there was a serious fault of which they appeared to be unaware and which, if not rectified, would lead to the removal of the lampstand.

Before we consider this, let us ask if the Master, looking at our ecclesias, could write to us in similar terms or would their standard of activity condemn us? Would he find an avoidance rather than an acceptance of toil, a love of ease and comfort rather than hard work? Would he find us ready to do the work which is seen of men and pleasant, and unwilling to accept the less obvious but equally necessary work of which few are aware? Would he find us willing to engage in the hard labour of Bible study—and it is hard labour if the result is to be profitable to the ecclesia—or would he see us hastily preparing an address a day or two before it is to be given? In an age of tolerance, would he find us rejecting those who would water down our beliefs and our way of life—perhaps trying to modify them to harmonise with modern thought? When we meet difficulties in the ecclesia or in the world, do we give up or do we face them with perseverance and fortitude?

There was, however, a serious fault at Ephesus. Endurance, unremitting toil and rejection of error are not all that the Lord requires. They are the means to an end: *"The aim of our charge is love that issues from a pure heart"* (1 Timothy 1:5). The Authorised Version wrongly softens the force of the Lord's rebuke by inserting "somewhat" in Revelation 2:4. Despite his praise, the Lord continued: *"But I have this against you, that you have abandoned the love you had at first"* (Revelation 2:4, R.S.V.) or *"you do not love as you did at first"* (Phillips). *"Remember then from what you have fallen. Repent and do the works you did at first. If not I will come to you and remove your lampstand from its place unless you repent"* (v. 5). The fault was so serious that it threatened the very existence of the ecclesia.

Jesus' reproof is often interpreted to mean that the ecclesia had lost its original zeal and enthusiasm. Such an understanding is inconsistent with the praise the Lord had just given, and he did not use the word for zeal or for enthusiasm but that for love, *agapē*. This word, or its cognate form, is used of the love of God for Jesus and the love of God and Jesus for us. It refers also to the love disciples have for one another which is the badge of true discipleship (John 13:35). They love one another as God, as Jesus, loves them. So the Lord prayed *"that the love with which thou (God) hast loved me, may be in them"* (John 17:26). His command to his disciples was *"Love one another,* **even as I have loved you***, that you also love one another"* (John 13:34). The supreme importance of this love in the believer's life was emphasised in the apostolic teaching and writings. *"You have been taught of God to love one another . . . do so more and more"* (1 Thessalonians 4:9). *"Make love your aim"* (1 Corinthians 14:1). *"Let all that you do be done in love"* (16:14). The love of Christ ought to control believers (2 Corinthians 5:14) so that *"through love (they) be servants of one another"* (Galatians 5:13), ready, if need be, to lay down their lives for the brethren as Jesus had done (1 John 3:16). Many similar passages might be quoted.

This love must be accompanied by good works. *"If anyone has the world's goods and sees his brother in need, yet closes his heart against him, how does God's love abide in him?"* (1 John 3:17).

This was part of the basic Christian teaching which had come to the brethren and sisters at Ephesus but they had also teaching specific to them. Paul in his letter to them prayed that they *"being rooted and grounded in love, may have power . . . to know the love of Christ"* which is beyond ordinary human knowledge (Ephesians 3:17-18). The reason for this prayer was that the love of Christ had to be their standard of behaviour in life. *"Husbands, love your wives* **as Christ also loved the Church** *and gave himself up for her"* (Ephesians 5:25). This standard applied not only to husbands but to them all. *"Walk in love,* **as Christ loved us***"* (5:2). This required them to forbear one another *in love* (4:2) and to speak the truth *in love* so that the ecclesia could build itself up *in love* (4:15-16).

Christian love is not what the world now (or then) calls love. It is not based on sentiment: we do not have to like people to love them in the New Testament sense. Love is something the Christian deliberately wills and expresses in actions done to all. The qualities of the love of Christ, or Christian love, are listed by

THE LETTER TO EPHESUS

Paul in 1 Corinthians 13. To help us understand the depth of meaning in those few verses, we set out in paraphrase some of the Apostle's points, based upon attempts by various translators to express the riches of Paul's words.

verse 4: *"Love is patient with people."* The word used by the Lord to describe the patient endurance of the ecclesia (*hupomonē*) is always used of patience with regard to things. A different word (*makrothumia*) here expresses patience with regard to persons.

"Love looks for a way of being constructive."

"There is no envy in love."

"Love is not boastful."

"Love is not forward or assertive." The word comes from a root meaning "windbag".

verse 5: *"Love gives itself no airs"* and *"never lacks courtesy."*

"Love does not insist on its own way; it is not irritable or resentful." The word translated "resentful" is taken from the keeping of accounts and refers to an entry in a ledger. Love does not keep a record of words or actions by which it is hurt so that these can be repaid in kind. Hence the translation *"does not keep an account of evil"*.

verse 6: *"Love finds nothing to be glad about when others go wrong, but rejoices in the truth."*

verse 7: *"Love can stand any kind of treatment"*, or *"is always slow to expose"*, *"always eager to believe the best, always hopes, always perseveres."*

verse 8: *"Love never ends."*

Here are the qualities of the love a true ecclesia must allow to control its communal life. This in turn requires that each individual member should show these in his or her own life. Love will, if we allow it, answer our personal and ecclesial problems.

For example, Paul repeatedly reproved the Corinthians for being "puffed up". (He only used the phrase once outside the first letter to the Corinthians.) There was partisanship at Corinth. *"Some say, 'I belong to Paul'; others, 'I follow Apollos'; others say, 'I am Peter's man'; and others again, 'I belong to Christ'—as though Christ had been divided up so as to belong to one party instead of to you all!"*

THE LETTERS TO THE SEVEN CHURCHES OF ASIA

(1 Corinthians 1:12-13, Bruce). They were puffed up in favour of one of those leaders as against the others (4:7); "arrogant" (4:18). They were likewise "puffed up" ("arrogant", R.S.V.) at the case of immorality so bad as to be unknown even among the pagans around them (5:1-2) and also puffed up by the knowledge of which some of them were so proud (8:1-2). Christian love is not puffed up nor arrogant and the Corinthians would cease to display these faults if they allowed this love to control their lives.

Eating things sacrificed to idols had become a problem at Corinth. We shall meet this in the letters to Pergamum and Thyatira. Suffice it now to say that some at Corinth claimed freedom of action which could harm some of their brethren and sisters. Paul's attitude was that he would refrain from eating meat offered to an idol if, so doing, he caused his brother to fall. Paul's instructions given at some length would have been unnecessary if love had ruled their lives because love is kind, and never places her own interests first.

There was a potentially divisive situation at Philippi when Paul wrote to the ecclesia there. Two sisters who had laboured side by side with Paul (R.S.V.), shared his toil (Weymouth) and been active in the ecclesia, were now at loggerheads. This was not the result of doctrinal differences but of the clash of two strong personalities which, uncorrected, would lead to factions as at Corinth and destroy the unity of the ecclesia. The apostle does not mention the cause of the quarrel but his language suggests that it could have resulted from differences of judgement on the best way of carrying on the work in Philippi. One sister may have tried to force changes on the ecclesia. She may have felt absolutely certain that what she proposed was for the good of the ecclesia and, therefore, she was justified in continuing to press for these changes to be made. The human heart can so easily camouflage what is basically a desire to have one's own way as being in the best interests of the Truth. The other sister may have been equally convinced that the proposed changes would not help the ecclesia. Whatever the details, the basic cause of the differences between the two sisters was a lack of humility, an unwillingness to concede that the other sister might, after all, be right, or

THE LETTER TO EPHESUS

to accept a decision that went against one or the other.

If Love is in Control

So Paul prefaced those sublime verses on the humility of Christ with these words: *"Do nothing from selfishness or conceit, but in humility count others better than yourselves. Let each of you look not only to his own interests, but also to the interests of others"* (Philippians 2:3-4). In those words Paul reminded the ecclesia of some of the qualities of love, which is not selfish, not conceited, not proud. The differences between the two sisters would wither and die if they allowed this love to control their words and actions. Again, *"Do all things without grumbling or questioning"* (2:14), or, *"Be ever on your guard against a grudging and contentious spirit"* (Weymouth). Here is an appeal to other of the qualities of love which has good manners (Phillips) and never shows bitterness or resentment (Wand). A final quotation: *"Let your moderation* ("forbearance", R.V. and R.S.V.; "gentleness", R.V.m.) *be known unto all men"* (4:5). The Greek word Paul used cannot be translated into English by one word. Trench says that it expresses that moderation which avoids the danger of such strong assertion of legal rights that these become moral wrongs, which refrains from pushing its own rights to the uttermost and withdraws in part or whole from these. This was the quality which would rectify the position at Philippi, where rights were being pressed so strongly. Paul is again asking the ecclesia to display the qualities of love which *"never places her own interests first"* (Bruce), *"never insists on its rights"* (Barclay), *"never pursues its own selfish interest"* (Wand). Christian love, if allowed to control their communal life, would resolve this dispute.

The early believers had to learn to allow this love to control their individual and communal lives (cf. Ephesians 4:31-32). They would inevitably fail but this love must increasingly dominate their lives. They had had a sad example of the failure to allow love to control the relationship between believers. Two of their best loved leaders had worked together for many years. Paul owed much to Barnabas who vouched for Paul when the Jerusalem ecclesia hesitated to receive him and who brought the apostle from Tarsus to Antioch to join the work which led to their joint missionary journey.

THE LETTERS TO THE SEVEN CHURCHES OF ASIA

When a second missionary journey was mooted, there was sharp dissension between them. Let us use our imagination. Barnabas wanted to take John Mark with them again, but Paul refused because Mark *"had deserted them in Pamphylia and was not prepared to go on with them in their work"* (Acts 15:38, Phillips). Barnabas would say that Mark had learned his lesson and, given an opportunity, would redeem himself. Paul would reply that the work was far too important to risk taking with them a man who had already let them down. He must not be given the opportunity to do so again and Barnabas would agree if Mark were not his cousin. Luke records that *"in irritation they parted company"* (Acts 15:39, Moffatt), and Paul used a cognate Greek word in describing one of the qualities of love which is "never irritated". May one suggest that Paul never forgot this failure in love. He and Barnabas had not been patient, they had been rude to one another and had insisted each on his own way. Paul had not thought the best of Mark. The effect on the infant churches could have been disastrous. Apart from the bad example set them, the dissension between Paul and Barnabas would give an excuse for partisanship such as Paul had deplored at Corinth.

The separation of Paul and Barnabas could easily lead the ecclesias to take sides and refuse to receive at the Lord's table one or other of the apostles. Thus, years later, Paul found it necessary to remind the ecclesia at Colossae that they had been instructed to receive Mark the cousin of Barnabas if he came to them and *"make him welcome"* (Colossians 4:10, Phillips). Mark did redeem himself. He later worked again with Paul (Colossians 4:10) and the apostle in his last letter asked Timothy to *"get Mark and bring him with you; for he is very useful in serving me"* (2 Timothy 4:11). Paul's earlier assessment of Mark had been proved wrong. He had not behaved to Mark with the kindness love required.

A Lost Love

This love had once been evident in the Ephesian ecclesia but was absent when the Lord wrote. Before we attempt to ascertain why the ecclesia ceased to display love, let us ask ourselves some questions.

How far does this love control our personal, ecclesial and communal lives? How much do we as individuals show these qualities of love in our lives? Do those with whom we come into contact in our daily work, or in other ways, see them in our lives so that they recognise us as followers of Jesus not only because we talk of him but by our manner of life? Do they see his love in our lives, in patience, in kindness, in courtesy and in the absence of jealousy, of self-conceit, irritability, and resentment? Do wives see these qualities in their husbands? Do our brethren and sisters see them in us in our communal life? These are vital questions because the absence of love among his people, in his ecclesias, the Lord will not pardon.

There is increasing emphasis in our community on good works to others—and rightly so, because such works are an essential part of the Christian life; but we must recognise that these are not necessarily acts of love. For example, it is possible to give away all we have and be without love. It is relatively easy to give food, drink or clothes to those in need, at home or abroad, to visit the sick and extend hospitality. It is very much more difficult to show the qualities of love in our lives in the ecclesias and in the community but if we do not, our "good works" will be valueless. *"On that day many will say to me, 'Lord, Lord, did we not prophesy in your name, and cast out demons in your name, and do many mighty works in your name?' And then will I declare to them, 'I never knew you'."* May we attempt to put the Lord's words in modern terms: 'Lord, did we not do much speaking in your name, spend many hours on your work?' Jesus will not acknowledge such unless they were done in love.

What does this mean in practice? Our communal life offers endless opportunities for the exercise of love. We shall each fail but our failure gives our brethren and sisters the opportunity to show the qualities of love, to be very patient and kind to us in our failures. They will not be rude to us, or irritated by us, nor will they impute bad motives for our actions. They will not be touchy but will have a poor memory for our weaknesses and be slow to talk about or expose them to others.

THE LETTERS TO THE SEVEN CHURCHES OF ASIA

These are among the facets of love we ought to display in our life in the ecclesia and in the brotherhood. They are not what we do by nature and their performance will tax us to the limit of our powers but we must always remember they are the badge of true disciples.

No Conscious Decision

Why had the ecclesia at Ephesus ceased to display love? It was the only community in the city in which the love of Christ could, and should have been seen. This love had once controlled their lives (cf. Ephesians 1:15) but had ceased so to do. The ecclesias at Pergamum and Thyatira must deliberately have decided to accept those who held the teaching of Balaam and of the Nicolaitans and to tolerate the woman Jezebel. The Ephesian brethren and sisters had not made a conscious decision, had not passed an ecclesial resolution to abandon love, but love can go gradually from an ecclesia or a community without those concerned being aware of it. This is what seems to have happened at Ephesus and the Lord's diagnosis would come as a tremendous shock, but they could not doubt it because it was the verdict of the One who walked in their midst.

"Take heed to yourselves"

Here was an ecclesia, almost certainly the largest in Asia, seen by other ecclesias as one of untiring labour and endurance where there was purity of doctrine and manner of life maintained by their rejection of teachers of error. The Ephesian ecclesia did not take their faith lightly and accepted that it made great demands on them. They had done their duty as they saw it and done it well. Ephesus would have been regarded by other ecclesias as a model meeting which left nothing to be desired. But what was not apparent to human eyes was that the true motive power was missing. The Lord had not been able to say to them, as Paul had to the Thessalonians, that their labour had been *"prompted by love"* (1 Thessalonians 1:3, N.I.V.).

Paul, on his way to Jerusalem shortly before his arrest there, put in at Miletus and summoned the elders of the Ephesian ecclesia to meet him there to receive his solemn charge: *"Take heed to yourselves and to all the flock, in which the Holy Spirit has made you guardians, to feed the church of the Lord which he obtained with his own blood. I know that after my departure fierce wolves will come in among you, not sparing the flock; and from among your own selves will men arise speaking perverse things to draw away disciples after them. Therefore be alert"* (Acts 20:28-31). The errors would be both in the things to be believed and in the manner of life which should result from these beliefs.

Contrary to his expectation at Miletus, Paul had been able to revisit Ephesus where he found, as he had foretold, that grievous wolves had entered the church. He met opposition there, probably connected with Jewish fables and matters concerning the Law (1 Timothy 1:4,7; cf. Titus 1:14). The errors at Ephesus seem to have spread throughout the province of Asia, causing Paul later to write that *"all who are in Asia turned away from me"* (2 Timothy 1:15). It is probable that Timothy, sent by Paul to Ephesus, did not stay there long (cf. 2 Timothy 4:9-13) and the elders of the ecclesia had to complete the difficult task he had begun. It was imperative for the survival, and more so the growth of the Truth in Asia, that the largest ecclesia in the province should be seen to be guarding the deposit successfully. The necessity for clear, well-grounded teaching was evident. They had contended for the faith which was once for all delivered to the saints (Jude 3); they had tested and exposed the grievous wolves, evil men and false apostles, who had entered the flock. This was a continuing process because scholars say that the tense the Lord used indicates that there had been a recent occasion when this had been necessary.

The spirit in which this contending and testing ought to have been done had been expressed in Paul's instructions to Timothy: *"The Lord's servant must not be quarrelsome but kindly to everyone, an apt teacher, forbearing, correcting his opponents with gentleness"* (2 Timothy 2:24-25; cf. 2 Corinthians 2:7-8). Notice here again, how the qualities of love were to control their actions, even their attitude to those in error, bearing in mind that *"God may perhaps grant that they will repent and come to know the truth"* (v. 25). Abandoning the love they once had meant that they ceased to be kind, gentle and forbearing and became quarrelsome. The testing of evil men and false apostles seems to have affected their attitude to one another and an inquisitorial spirit developed in the ecclesia which led to mistrust and suspicion. Every word and action was subjected to intense scrutiny to ensure that they each were free from any suspicion of error.

Under such conditions it is easy to make a man an offender for a word but in such an atmosphere love withers and dies, with the consequent disappearance of the qualities of kindness, patience and forbearance Paul inculcated (Ephesians 4:31-32). Their intention to preserve the deposit in its purity was entirely laudable; the irony, the tragedy was that the way they did this, although preserving the manner of life from immoral influences, emphasised its negative aspects and removed the positive quality, the supreme crown of the Christian life, love. They had preserved the church of the Lord from error but they had failed to feed it.

It is not without interest that the trade guilds at Ephesus suffered from fractiousness and rancour. Thus, a pagan philosopher, not long after the Lord's letter, emphasised the need for amity in these guilds. This attitude in the city may have been a factor in the instruction Paul had earlier given the ecclesia to maintain the unity of the Spirit in the bond of peace, to attain the unity of the faith, to be joined and knit together (Ephesians 4:3,13,16). Had the ecclesia allowed this characteristic of the pagan society out of which they had come, but in which they still had to live and work, to influence their attitude to one another?

Later letters to the seven ecclesias show the danger of compromise to which these early ecclesias appear to have been more susceptible than to the failings at Ephesus. It is difficult to preserve the deposit without on the one hand emphasising purity of belief and life in such a way that love is lost and on the other hand compromising and destroying these.

There is here a lesson for modern believers. If the Ephesian ecclesia, despite the emphasis on love in the apostolic teaching,

THE LETTER TO EPHESUS

especially in the writings particular to Ephesus*, could nonetheless lose love, 20th century ecclesias should carefully examine themselves. The ecclesias to which we belong may appear to others to be model ecclesias, as did Ephesus, leaving little to be desired, but if they lack love they are nothing. Again like the Ephesian meeting, modern ecclesias may be unconscious of this deficiency. Our Lord does not write direct to our ecclesias today but his letter to Ephesus has enabled believers in all subsequent ages to examine themselves through his eyes and ascertain if true love crowns their lives.

Doctrine and Love

The Truth was recovered with great effort in the last century and the need for clear, well-grounded teaching was as apparent then as it had been at Ephesus. Understandably and rightly, great emphasis was laid on the Statement of Faith which defined the first principles of the teaching believers held in common. Zeal for the maintenance of the purity of the Faith is essential but it can be expressed in harsh, biting words not inspired by love. We sometimes act as if the deposit can only be guarded by being rude to one another.

We must always remember that the things to be believed are part only of what the New Testament calls "doctrine" which, in our modern parlance, is a combination of the Statement of Faith and the Commandments of Christ. Belief in the Statement of Faith is valueless if it does not control our words and actions, our manner of life. We must not so emphasise the importance of sound doctrine that we forget the love which should issue from it.

This is not a plea for laxity but for a balanced attitude. Some of the evils listed by Paul (1 Timothy 1:10) are evident in the world around us and we cannot fellowship any who refuse to forsake such, nor can we receive those who do not believe the things concerning the Kingdom of God and the name of Jesus Christ. But in discharging this duty, we must speak the truth in love, remembering that all that we do ought to be done in love, that we

---

*Compare The Letter to Laodicea, under "How the Gospel came to Laodicea", p. 105.

should always have in mind *"how to stir up one another to love and to good works"* (Hebrews 10:24). The dividing line between loss of love on the one hand and compromise on the other is as fine and as difficult to draw now as in the first century.

Nor must we judge the elders at Ephesus harshly. Had the Arranging Brethren of a modern ecclesia—our own—been summoned by Paul to receive a charge similar to that given to the Ephesian elders, they might well have reacted as did their first century counterparts. The Lord's letter to Ephesus was written so that we can profit from their mistake. It is difficult simultaneously to condemn the sin and be compassionate to the sinner. The perfect example here, as in all other ways, is our Lord but we must never forget his instruction to penitents to go and sin no more. They had truly to change their way of life.

Repentance is Urgent

The Lord now reminds the Ephesian ecclesia of this need. First, they must remember how far they had fallen. The tense of the Greek word used implies "keep on remembering". They would then repent, change their manner of life to live as they had at first, allowing love to control their words and actions. Failure to do so would result in the removal of the lightstand, notwithstanding their toil and endurance. The Lord would be unable to continue to recognise them as his because an ecclesia which does not shed the light of love into the darkness around it has lost the reason for its existence. Repentance was urgent. The tense of the Lord's words indicates a near visitation in judgement if they failed to return to the first works and become again a community of men and women who loved one another. We too shall fail, however arduous our labours, however strong our zeal for purity, if the love of Christ cannot be seen at work in our ecclesias and brotherhood.

The Lord continued: *"Yet this you have, that you hate the works of the Nicolaitans, which I also hate"* (v. 6). This letter is the only one of the seven in which commendation is added after a warning and this was done because the Lord did not wish them to draw the wrong conclusion from his rebuke. They were right to hate the

THE LETTER TO EPHESUS

works of the Nicolaitans and he did not wish the ecclesia to desist from so doing, or from testing *"the spirits to see whether they are of God"* (1 John 4:1). Love must not reduce their hatred of error or immoral behaviour. The Nicolaitans are mentioned again in the letter to Pergamum and we will defer consideration of them until we come to that letter. Suffice it to say now that they appear to have been people whose immoral lives were inconsistent with their profession of the Truth. Notice the Lord's phraseology. It was the works of the Nicolaitans, not the Nicolaitans themselves, which were hated. God hates evil actions (Isaiah 61:8; Amos 5:21; Zechariah 8:16-17) and believers do likewise (cf. Jude 23) but without rancour or malice towards the evildoers themselves.

Lessons for all the Ecclesias

The Lord concludes thus: *"He who has an ear, let him hear what the Spirit says to the churches. To him who conquers I will grant to eat of the tree of life, which is in the paradise of God"* (v. 7). Jesus there states clearly that the letter was not solely for the Ephesian ecclesia but for all the churches that each might profit from it. All who hear must appropriate to themselves and to their ecclesias the warnings and promises made to the seven churches.

The words "He who has an ear, let him hear" often occur in our Lord's words recorded in the Gospels, usually to emphasise an important statement (e.g. Matthew 11:15; 13:9,43; Mark 4:9,23). Here they introduce the reward promised in the first three letters but follow it in the last four. Thus the three "ports", Ephesus, Smyrna and Pergamum form one group within the seven, and the four hinterland ecclesias, Thyatira, Sardis, Philadelphia and Laodicea another. The links between all seven ecclesias must have been close because, during Paul's work in Ephesus, *"all the residents of Asia heard the words of God, both Jews and Greeks"* (Acts 19:10). Ephesus would therefore have been to some extent the mother church of the other ecclesias but there is perhaps a hint in the grouping that the relationship between Ephesus, Smyrna and Pergamum was especially close. Again, the Lord told each of the last four ecclesias, *"I know your works"*, whereas in the first group Ephesus only is thus addressed. It is as though the links between the group of three were so close that what was said in the introduction of the letter to Ephesus would be taken as applying to the other two and would automatically become known to them. We do not know but we shall be able to find out if we are permitted to be in God's Kingdom.

A reward was promised to those who conquer, who overcome, who endure to the end (Matthew 24:13). In the world they might have tribulation but the promise to them came from the One who had overcome the world (John 16:33). We shall leave consideration of the reward until the final chapter when we shall consider the promises to all the ecclesias.

Guarding the Deposit Committed to Us

In conclusion, let us summarise what we have learned from the letter to Ephesus. The Lord sees us as we really are. He knows if we are carefully guarding the deposit committed to us, if we are labouring for him to the utmost of our powers, if we are enduring patiently and bearing up for his name's sake. There may be times in our lives when we feel that the difficulties we face are such that we just cannot carry on. Then is the time to consider him who for us endured from sinners such hostility against himself (Hebrews 12:3) and realise that neither our problems nor our weaknesses are sufficient cause for us to give up. Thus Paul was *"afflicted in every way, but not crushed; perplexed, but not driven to despair; persecuted but not forsaken; struck down but not destroyed"* (2 Corinthians 4:8-9). So we, remembering that we are in the hand of the One from whom none can pluck us, not merely endure but bear up for his name's sake.

Above all, the Lord knows if his love is increasingly present among us. We have been shown both the qualities and the paramount importance of this love in our lives as individuals, and in the ecclesias and brotherhood and that nothing can compensate for its absence.

4

THE LETTER TO SMYRNA

SMYRNA, situated about 35 miles north of Ephesus, was one of the greatest and wealthiest cities in the Roman province of Asia. A city had existed at Smyrna for many centuries before Christ but it had been destroyed about 600 B.C. The city was rebuilt in the 4th century B.C. after the conquests of Alexander the Great. It had been well laid out in rectangular blocks with wide streets and was a model of the town planner's art. Smyrna had become the most brilliant and splendid of the cities of Asia and was known as the ornament or glory of Asia.

The city had sided with Rome long before the latter became a world power and, when John wrote, had been her faithful ally for almost three centuries. In 196 B.C. Smyrna had been the first city in the world outside Rome to erect a temple to Roma, the goddess of Rome. In A.D. 26 Smyrna successfully competed with the major cities of Asia, including Ephesus and Sardis, for the right to erect a temple to the god Tiberius, the reigning emperor. Emperor worship was at first frowned upon by the emperors, but they later realised the advantages which could accrue from it and by the time John wrote it was compulsory for all the subject peoples of the empire. Rome tolerated the many gods worshipped by its subjects provided they added the worship of the Emperor to that of their other gods. This they had no difficulty in doing. The benefit to Rome of Emperor worship was that it was the one thing all its subjects had in common and thus helped to unify the various races of the empire.

It had become a test of loyalty to Rome. People burned incense on the altar dedicated to the Emperor and called him "lord". Refusal to do so marked the person as a traitor or rebel worthy of death. Rome had exempted the Jews from this test but the

THE LETTERS TO THE SEVEN CHURCHES OF ASIA

Christians lost this immunity once Rome ceased to regard them as a Jewish sect. They could not burn incense on Caesar's altar and say "Caesar is Lord" because they called Jesus "Lord" and refused to give the title to any other man. For this reason Christians throughout the empire were liable to persecution from the authorities. This was particularly so in Smyrna which, intensely loyal to Rome and a centre of Emperor worship, would be expected vigorously to apply this test of loyalty to Rome. Informers, Jewish or pagan, incited the authorities against the believers. This was especially true of Jews who, themselves exempt from this test of loyalty, could easily use it or incite its use against the brethren and sisters. Christianity in Smyrna was a dangerous profession often resulting in death by burning, crucifixion or wild beasts.

The guardian deity of Smyrna was a local version of the mother goddess Cybele, known as the Siphylene Mother but many other gods were also worshipped. Smyrna was the special home of the cult of Dionysus, the god of wine, later called Bacchus by the Romans whose worship was accompanied by drunkenness and sexual immorality. One writer said that the festivals in honour of Bacchus "were among the most debasing and demoralizing spectacles which heathendom ever introduced, and contributed greatly to the corruption of morals among all ranks of the people" (Tait, *Messages to the Seven Churches*, p. 184).

Jewish Incitement

Attracted by the opportunities for trade in a city of 140,000 inhabitants a large number of Jews had settled in Smyrna and were bitterly hostile to the Christians. The Acts of the Apostles gives examples from the earliest days of the church of this hostility and Jewish incitement of their pagan neighbours against the apostles (Acts 13-19). About 60 years after John wrote, Polycarp was burned to death in Smyrna for his profession of Christianity. The Jews of the city took a prominent part in his execution on a Saturday afternoon in the stadium where games were being held. Normally the Jews would not have entered the stadium when games were in progress but such was their hatred of the brethren

THE LETTER TO SMYRNA

that they not only did so but profaned the Sabbath by bringing and arranging the faggots with which Polycarp was burned.

There were several reasons for the Jewish antagonism to the believers. The episode of Polycarp suggests that some at least of the Jews in the city had succumbed to the temptations of the society in which they lived and no longer maintained the old Jewish standards of purity and separateness. Jews who disapproved of this laxity would be attracted by the high moral standards of Christianity. Further, the Acts of the Apostles states that many early converts came from those called "godfearers", who were Gentiles attracted by the monotheism and moral teaching of Judaism, and attended the synagogues but did not become proselytes because they were unwilling to accept circumcision and the strict Jewish dietary laws.

The Jews themselves were missionaries—they traversed sea and land to make a single proselyte (Matthew 23:15)—and the defection of their converts or near converts to Christianity would be galling to them. They were punctilious in their observance of the Jewish law and contributed regularly to the upkeep of the temple, going up to feasts there (Acts 2). Relations between them and the Palestinian Jews were thus close and cordial and although they remained loyal to Rome during the revolt of A.D. 66-70, they must have been deeply affected by the sack of the Temple. The attitude of the Christians toward this and the observances of the law would inflame Jewish feeling against the Christian brotherhood, already intense because of its teaching that a carpenter crucified as a criminal was indeed the Jewish Messiah, God's Son and that the brotherhood was now the true Israel of God.

Unmitigated Praise

With this background, we come to the Letter to Smyrna (Revelation 2:8-11): it is wholly commendatory, the most laudatory of the seven epistles. The brethren and sisters had been untouched by the drunkenness and licentiousness which accompanied the festivals in honour of Bacchus. The tribulation they experienced had helped to maintain purity of life because there could be no compromise with a society which persecuted and despoiled them. Here is an example for modern believers. A major problem in the society in which we live is the misuse, rather, the abuse of alcohol. This is especially prevalent in young people and is a cause of violence and immorality but it is not confined to teenagers. There are hundreds of thousands of adults in the United Kingdom with alcoholism, among them businessmen and women of middle age. Believers today cannot avoid living in such a society but they must follow the example of their predecessors at Smyrna and be separate from it, not sharing this characteristic. Believers today, as then, are required to live sober, upright and godly lives while awaiting their Lord's coming.

"I know your tribulation." The basic meaning of the word is pressure, for example, the pressure exerted by a tightly fitting shoe on the foot. It is used metaphorically in the New Testament of tribulation, the heavy pressures to which believers were subjected because of their profession of Christ. The Lord knew the pressure on this ecclesia. He continues: *"I know your poverty."* This is the only letter in which the poverty of believers in this world's goods is mentioned.

The True Riches

The word translated "poverty" (*ptōcheia*) denotes extreme poverty, destitution, and indicates people without worldly possessions. The brethren and sisters were barely able to provide the absolute necessities of life. It is true that God has chosen those who are poor in the world (James 2:5) so that none might boast in His presence (1 Corinthians 1:29) but it seems improbable that this was the sole cause of their poverty in such a wealthy city. The coupling of tribulation and poverty makes it much more likely that their poverty was aggravated by, if not wholly due to, rampaging mobs who plundered their goods in the tribulation which had come on them (Hebrews 10:34). The word *ptōcheia* is used of the Lord himself who became poor that by his poverty they might become rich. The one who had not where to lay his head not only knew but understood from his own experience the poverty of his people in Smyrna because he had experienced similar poverty.

A delightful parenthesis follows: *"(but you are rich)"*. Robbed of their material possessions, they were nevertheless *"rich toward God"* (Luke 12:21); *"rich in good deeds"* (1 Timothy 6:18); *"rich in faith"* (James 2:5). Human and divine assessments are here contrasted. Men saw only an impoverished persecuted community but the Lord saw an ecclesia which had laid up for itself treasures in heaven where neither moth nor rust consume and where thieves do not break in and steal (Matthew 6:20).

This true wealth was beyond the reach of plundering hands. Note that there is no hint that the brethren and sisters complained of their poverty; they did not covet what they had lost. Their spirit had not been soured by their experiences. The condition of this ecclesia was the exact opposite of that in Laodicea, which thought itself rich, prosperous and needing nothing, whereas in the Lord's eyes they were wretched, pitiable, poor, blind and naked (Revelation 3:17). How the Lord's assessment must have cheered the ecclesia at Smyrna! Today we in the West live in a materialistic society and have possessions undreamed of even half a century ago. These can tempt us to make the acquisition of material things our main aim in life so that we fail to be rich in those qualities which constitute real wealth in our Lord's sight. We shall have more to say about this when we come to the Letter to Laodicea.

False Accusers

The Lord also knew the slander, the defamation of those who said they were Jews but were not, and had forgotten the manner of life appropriate to those who claimed to be God's people. The Greek is said to indicate that the calumnies were not only uttered by the Synagogue of Satan but originated with them and were probably repeated among the pagans. How easy it would be to inform against believers, laying a charge of sedition before the Romans because the Christian believed in another King, one Jesus (Acts 17:7).

How easy also to traduce the Christian way of life with its separation from society and heathen customs. Again, Jesus not only knew but understood what his brethren and sisters were undergoing because he too had experienced the hostility of the synagogue, and had been defamed by those who falsely claimed to be true Jews. Gentiles had been incited against the Lord to bring about his death on a charge of treason, just as Jews in Smyrna roused the Gentile mob against his ecclesia there. The word "synagogue" means an assembly or gathering and is repeatedly used in the Septuagint (LXX) in this sense. The official title of a synagogue at this time was "The Synagogue of the Lord", taken from the Old Testament (e.g. Numbers 20:4 and 31:16, LXX) but the synagogue at Smyrna had become a synagogue of the adversary, Jews after the flesh persecuting those after the spirit.

"Be faithful unto death"

The difficulties at Smyrna would increase but before telling the brethren and sisters of things to come, the Lord encouraged them: *"Do not fear what you are about to suffer."* "Do not fear." Those words were often on their Lord's lips during his ministry. They were spoken to Jairus to sustain his faith when the ruler of the synagogue was told that his daughter was dead and there was therefore no point in troubling Jesus any more (Mark 5:36). They were uttered by Jesus to the disciples in the boat when they were terrified as they saw him walking on the water to them (Mark 6:50; cf. 4:40). They had recently been spoken by the glorified Jesus when the beloved disciple fell at his Lord's feet as though dead and now to brethren and sisters who after their traumatic experiences must have been wondering, if not apprehensive, as to what the future held for them. They were not promised that life would be easy and pleasant. On the contrary, Jesus did not hide from them that worse was to come but sought to strengthen their faith with these words so pregnant with meaning:

> *"Behold, the devil* (the false accuser, the combination of Jew and Gentile) *is about to throw some of you into prison that you may be tested, and for ten days you will have tribulation. Be faithful* (prove yourselves faithful) *unto death."*

The word "Behold" in the Greek is emphatic—"Behold for certain". The coming tribulation was inescapable but its purpose was clearly stated; it was to test them, to determine if they would be loyal to Jesus even at the cost of life itself, if they would hold fast the confession of their faith to the bitter end without wavering (Hebrews 10:23). How easy it would have been for a persecuted church to feel forgotten and forsaken, to abandon the unequal conflict and free itself from poverty and tribulation by burning incense on the Emperor's altar and acknowledging him as lord!

And how appropriate to this situation were the words with which Jesus introduced himself to his people living under the shadow of death! He too had been tested to the limit but had kept his faith in his Father even to the death of the cross and, although he died, had come to life again and now lives for ever. The promise to them was not that they would escape death but that, like their Lord, they would live again for ever. Despite the persecution and death that awaited them, life, victory over death is the keynote of the letter.

And how closely Jesus identified himself with the ecclesia and his experience with those of his brethren and sisters! The Lord knew the difficulties about to come on them but, much more important to them, he could enter into the feelings of his brethren and sisters when tested because he himself had been tested by similar but even greater pressures in his life on earth. The ecclesia was not asked to prove its loyalty to a leader remote from their problems and without real understanding of them but to one who had in every respect been tempted, tested as they would be and who could therefore sympathise with them in their tribulation.

The Lord was not only the one who died and came to life but *"the first and the last"*. God described Himself in the Old Testament as the first and the last (Isaiah 44:6; 48:12). This divine title had been given to Jesus, indicating that all power in heaven and earth was now his and therefore none could pluck them from his hand or separate them from his love.

Some of them would be thrown into prison. Imprisonment was not normally used by the Romans as a punishment as it is today. Prison was much more the place of detention before trial or between trial and punishment which in their case would be death if they refused to deny Christ and worship the Emperor. A word of comfort followed. The tribulation would last ten days, a phrase probably used to denote a relatively short period (cf. Daniel 1:12; Genesis 24:55). The tribulation would test them to the uttermost but it would be for a time only. Endure it, prove yourselves faithful unto death and I will give you the crown of life. As with the Letter to Ephesus, we defer consideration of that promise until the final chapter.

What relevance has this letter to brethren and sisters in the western world today? Believers have been persecuted from the first century onwards, even to the nineteenth century when the Truth was revived. In 1889 Brother J. Bland could write of ostracism in society and injury to business. But religious toleration has progressively increased since the first world war and there is little if any persecution today in the English-speaking world. What meaning can a letter exhorting to fidelity to Christ even at the cost of life itself have for us today?

Preparing for the Day of Trouble

Scripture is clear and emphatic in its teaching that the Lord's return will be preceded by an unprecedented time of trouble, causing distress of nations with no way out of their problems. We need not speculate on the precise developments which will cause this. It is sufficient for us to know that there will be a period of such intense tribulation before the Lord returns, that unless it were shortened for the elect's sake, no flesh would be saved.

We tell our friends of the coming of this time of trouble but we often seem to act as though our pleasant manner of life will continue until our Lord comes and we enter the Kingdom with him. This is not what Scripture teaches. If we believe that his return is imminent, we must also accept that this time of trouble is even nearer. When we read Brother Alan Eyre's book, *The Protesters*, or learn of religious persecution behind the Iron Curtain, we cannot but wonder how we would react to similar experiences. Would we remain faithful? This question is one we, especially the younger among us, may have to answer. We ought now to be preparing ourselves to meet this day of trouble because those of

THE LETTER TO SMYRNA

us living when it comes will be affected, severely tested by this great tribulation. Profession of Christ may come to involve great hardship and even cost life itself. The relevance of this letter as we prepare for such a time is clear. It is for us to use it to make ourselves ready.

Believers today may feel that something is lacking in their lives because they do not have to suffer for the name of Jesus, but tribulation is not the only test of loyalty to our Lord. Some of the other ecclesias not subject to persecution were, as we shall see later, compromising with the society in which they lived, even becoming permeated with its spirit and succumbing to immorality, or were badly neglecting the Lord's work and these were testing their fidelity to Jesus. The verb the Lord used for "tested" (*peirazō*) " signified the trying, intentionally, and with the purpose of discovering what of good or evil, of power or weakness, was in a person or thing" (Trench, *Synonyms of the New Testament*, p. 280). Thus it is used when the Pharisees tested Jesus (Matthew 16:1 etc.) and in the LXX when God tested Abraham (Genesis 22:1), Israel (Exodus 16:4 etc.) and Hezekiah (2 Chronicles 32:31).

Modern disciples cannot hope to escape tests to ascertain if they will put God before their families, as Abraham did, to determine if they will walk in God's law or not, as Israel were proved, or even, as with Hezekiah, to ascertain all that is in their hearts. Remember how Joseph and David were tested by sexual temptation, Job by material losses and ill-health, and so on.

Tried and Tested

Thus Peter wrote that believers may *"now for a little while . . . have to suffer grief in all kinds of trials"* (1 Peter 1:6, N.I.V.). Notice again the comfort given Peter: the trials were for a little while (cf. 5:10). The word translated trials is the noun corresponding to the verb Jesus used and refers to the tests by which the loyalty of God's people is determined. These tests, Peter continues, come *"so that the genuineness of your faith, more precious than gold which though perishable is tested by fire, may redound to praise and glory and honour at the revelation of Jesus Christ"* (v. 7). The word translated "tested", as gold tested by fire, is not the same word as the Lord used. It means to test, examine, to see whether a thing is genuine or not. It is used in the LXX for the proving of a precious metal which was tested by being subjected to intense heat. The molten metal, if pure, gave a clear surface but, if contaminated by base metals, showed a scum on its surface. Silver and gold were purified or prepared from their ores by subjection to intense heat and careful removal of the scum until only pure molten precious metal remained. This process is often used in the Old Testament as a figure by which God proved the metal of His people. Just one example: *"As silver and gold are tried (dokimazō) in the furnace, so are choice hearts with the Lord"* (Proverbs 17:3, LXX).

The Psalmist prays that this proving, assaying process might be carried out on him. *"Prove (dokimazō) me, O Lord, and try (peirazō) me; purify as with fire my reins and my heart"* (Psalm 26:2, LXX). David asked for his innermost thoughts to be thrown, as it were, into the refiner's crucible so that the dross in them may be removed leaving only pure gold, the proven, tried character pleasing to God. David's failure with regard to Uriah and Bathsheba shows how necessary was his prayer. We are so conscious of the dross in our characters that we shrink from repeating David's prayer, but none of us can escape the process described in it. If gold, which man values so highly, is tested by fire, how much more the faith of the Christian! Peter realised that the tests used, even if they did not involve physical suffering as persecution does, can nevertheless be very unpleasant, and cause grief; but they were unavoidable if God's purpose in believers was to be realised. This is true of believers of every generation, whether or not they suffer persecution for their Lord's name.

Faith Refined

Peter wrote of the genuineness (*dokimion*) of their faith. The meaning of this word was not understood until it was found in the papyri, where it has the meaning of "what is genuine". So the opening words of 1 Peter 1:7 are: *"so that what is genuine in your faith may be found more precious than gold"* (Deissmann, *Bible Studies*, p. 259). "What is genuine in your faith" means that which

THE LETTER TO SMYRNA

remains as pure metal after the dross has been purged away. Note the comfort in Peter's words, which imply that the tests are made in the expectation that there will be a residuum of purified metal. The refiner does not put ore into the refining pot, except in the belief that it will give a worthwhile yield of pure gold. Similarly, the tests to which the Divine refiner subjects His people are done in the expectation that, however much dross has to be removed, a refined character will ultimately remain which will be beyond price in the day of Christ. In verse 6, the apostle described the tests by which God proves His people as "various". The original word is *poikilos* which means, primarily, many coloured or variegated. The word is used in the LXX to describe the coat of many colours which Jacob gave Joseph (Genesis 37:3,23,32) and the precious stones of many colours David provided for the Temple (1 Chronicles 29:2). The trials which come to Christians are varied. Not all are subjected to the same proofs and the tests will vary from time to time in our lives. Our temperaments and the weaknesses which need eradication are as varied as the trials we experience.

The Message for the Ecclesia Today

What, then, are the messages which come from this letter to us today?

First, a wealthy ecclesia is not necessarily rich before God. A poor ecclesia, struggling to maintain its witness to Christ, may be rich in His sight.

Second, despite their abject poverty, their tribulation and the defamation to which the ecclesia was subject, the brethren and sisters had not grumbled about their lot or been provoked against their persecutors and traducers but had allowed love to control their words and actions. How delighted they must have been that the Lord could praise them without reservation, despite their sorry condition in the eyes of the citizens of Smyrna.

Third, and most important of all, their Lord understood their difficulties and could enter into their feelings because He had been tested and subjected to pressures similar to but even greater

THE LETTERS TO THE SEVEN CHURCHES OF ASIA

than those the ecclesia experienced. All power was now his and none could separate them from him.

We are all subjected in our everyday lives to tests which will show if we will be loyal to Jesus under all circumstances. Persecutions may at some time be added to these. Tests of whatever kind are not pleasant but we must remember when undergoing them that our Lord has been tested, tempted in every way that we are. We serve a Master not only of infinite power but of infinite understanding.

5

THE LETTER TO PERGAMOS

PERGAMOS, or Pergamum, as it is now generally called, was situated about three miles north of the river Caikos, some 15 miles from the sea and 58 miles from Smyrna. The city stood on a large rocky hill 1000 feet high which dominated the fertile and beautiful plain of the river. The houses were on the lower slopes of the hill and the temples and public buildings were erected on terraces cut out of the higher part of the hill, which therefore appeared to be covered with pagan temples and shrines. The temples were more magnificent than any in the province, with the sole exception of the temple of Diana in Ephesus. Shortly after John wrote, the Roman governor Pliny said that Pergamum was the most illustrious city of Asia. Ramsay has written that beyond all other sites in Asia Minor, Pergamum gives the traveller the impression of permanence, strength, authority and great size. In short, it was a royal city.

A City of Wealth and Culture

Pergamum became the capital of a wealthy kingdom following the break-up of Alexander the Great's empire. The kingdom of Pergamum was founded in 282 B.C. and a century or so later its King began to form a library which ultimately contained 200,000 volumes. This was done in rivalry with the famous library of Alexandria and to make Pergamum a centre of learning. The Pergamum library was later transferred to Alexandria by Mark Antony to please Cleopatra. The word "parchment" comes from Latin words meaning "paper of Pergamum". Made from skins, it is said to have been invented when Egypt banned the export of papyrus, the normal writing material, to Pergamum.

In 133 B.C. Attalus III bequeathed the Kingdom to the Romans, who formed it into the province of Asia. The city itself was for 2½ centuries the official capital of the province, where the Roman governor, the pro-consul of Asia, resided and from whence his power was exercised. Thus, when John wrote, Pergamum had been the seat of supreme authority over a large area for almost four centuries. As we saw in the introductory chapter, because of its geographical position, Pergamum could not compete with Ephesus and Smyrna as a centre of international commerce but it remained the official capital and the seat of Roman authority for decades after John wrote.

Pergamum contained more temples and cults than Ephesus. The pagan religions there were an amalgam of three main types: Emperor-worship, the old Asiatic gods, and those introduced by the Greeks. In 29 B.C. a temple was dedicated to the Roman emperor Augustus 50 years before that dedicated to Tiberius was built at Smyrna. As befitted the seat of Roman authority in the province, the emperor-cult was extremely strong. The most popular of the other deities worshipped were Dionysus (or Bacchus), the god of wine, Aesculapius the god of healing, whose symbol was a serpent, Zeus and Athena the goddess of wisdom and the arts. Both Aesculapius and Zeus were called *Sotēr*, the Saviour.

A Seat of Pagan Worship

The temple of Athena was built on the steep hill and beneath it, some 800 feet above the plain, was a magnificent altar to Zeus which stood on a base about 100 feet square. It was surmounted on three sides by colonnades and approached on the western side by a broad staircase. A frieze of sculpture 150 yards in length and depicting the Battle of the Giants, adorned the base (Pittman, *Words and Their Ways in the Greek New Testament*, p. 126). This altar was one of the wonders of the ancient world. Nevertheless, the most important deity was Aesculapius, whose worship brought much wealth to the city. The cult of Aesculapius was carried from Greece to Pergamum during the 4th century B.C. and in time his temple in Pergamum became the second most renowned health centre in the world, called by one writer the Lourdes of the province of Asia. In addition to the famous medical school

THE LETTER TO PERGAMOS

associated with the god's worship, there were also soothsaying, magic, sorcery and chicanery. Much wealth was brought into the city by people seeking cures at his shrine for all kinds of illness. Pergamum has been described as a combination of a pagan cathedral city, a university town and a royal residence. The pagan worship there was extremely licentious and some festivals in honour of the gods were so obscene that the Senate banned their observance in Rome. Even the capital, not renowned for its moral behaviour, could not tolerate them.

"I know where you dwell"

With this background, let us read the Lord's letter to the ecclesia in the city:

> *"And to the angel of the church in Pergamum write: The words of him who has the sharp two-edged sword. I know where you dwell, where Satan's throne is; you hold fast my name and you did not deny my faith even in the days of Antipas my witness, my faithful one, who was killed among you, where Satan dwells. But I have a few things against you: you have some there who hold the teaching of Balaam, who taught Balak to put a stumbling block before the sons of Israel, that they might eat food sacrificed to idols and practise immorality. So you also have some who hold the teaching of the Nicolaitans. Repent then. If not, I will come to you soon and war against them with the sword of my mouth. He who has an ear, let him hear what the Spirit says to the churches. To him who conquers I will give some of the hidden manna, and I will give him a white stone, with a new name written on the stone which no one knows except him who receives it"* (Revelation 2:12-17).

Note first the attribute the Lord selected from his description in Revelation 1 to introduce his letter: *"him who hath the sharp two-edged sword."* Two ideas are involved. *"The word of God is living and active, sharper than any two-edged sword, piercing to the division of soul and spirit, of joints and marrow, and discerning the thoughts and intentions of the heart. And before him no creature is hidden, but all are open and laid bare to the eyes of him with whom we have to do"* (Hebrews 4:12-13). Everything which concerned the ecclesia and each individual member was known to the Lord. But the concept of judgement is also involved: *"He is called ... the Word of God ... From his*

THE LETTERS TO THE SEVEN CHURCHES OF ASIA

mouth issues a sharp sword with which to smite the nations" (Revelation 19:13,15). As we shall see, judgement is not limited to the nations.

Notice especially how the Lord continued. In five of the other letters, he said *"I know your works"*. This was not said to Smyrna or to Pergamum. To Smyrna the Lord had said, *"I know your tribulation and your poverty"*, and to Pergamum, *"I know where you dwell, where Satan's throne is"*. In each case, the Lord began by assuring the ecclesias that he was fully cognisant of the particular difficulties and dangers they faced. The One before whom all things are open and laid bare knew that his ecclesia in Pergamum lived and witnessed for him in a city where Satan's throne was. The word "dwell" means to settle and denotes a permanent rather than a temporary residence. The brethren and sisters were not nomads who could escape from their difficulties by moving away from the city. They had not chosen to live there as Lot had selected Sodom. They had probably met the Truth in Pergamum —how we do not know—and the difficulties they encountered in witnessing to Jesus were especially great because Satan's throne was there.

"The Throne of Satan"

The word "throne" (*thrŏnos*) is used in the New Testament to denote the seat of authority. The primary reference, therefore, was to Pergamum as the seat of Roman authority, where worship of the Emperor as the test of loyalty to Rome would be rigidly enforced. Antipas had probably been executed because he refused to offer incense on Caesar's altar and call him Lord. Here the adversary who wielded the power of life and death had used this power against Antipas, but there may also be some reference in the phrase "the throne of Satan" to the strength of paganism in Pergamum, to the title of Saviour given to some of the pagan gods and to the serpent as a symbol of Aesculapius. In this city were concentrated the power and seduction of the adversary whom the brethren and sisters had to face.

Commendation follows: *"You hold fast my name and you did not deny my faith even in the days of Antipas, my witness, my faithful one,*

THE LETTER TO PERGAMOS

who was killed among you, where Satan dwells." Notice the repetition of the words "where Satan dwells".

The brethren and sisters at Pergamum were faced with problems and dangers probably greater than in any other of the seven cities. The Lord by this repetition emphasised to them his complete knowledge and understanding of their problems. The Gospels show how these qualities were manifested in our Lord's life on earth, and the glorified Lord retained them. No further particulars are given regarding Antipas. He was probably the first believer in Pergamum, possibly in the province itself, to be executed for his faith. This could well have indicated a change in State policy towards Christians and be a foretaste of difficulties ahead as Rome increasingly insisted that all should prove their loyalty by emperor worship. Notice how the Lord tried to strengthen them. We have seen how the Lord identified himself with the ecclesia at Smyrna. Now he did the same with Antipas. The Greek words used of Jesus as *"the faithful witness"* (Revelation 1:5) are applied by the Lord to Antipas with the addition of "my". (*Martys* is translated "witness" in the R.S.V. in all but one of its occurrences in the New Testament. When John wrote, the word was probably only beginning to acquire our meaning of martyr.)

Faithful Witnesses

The repetition of "my"—*my* witness, *my* faithful one—emphasised the Lord's identification of himself with his faithful witness. Jesus, having witnessed a good confession before Pontius Pilate at the cost of his life (1 Timothy 6:13), acknowledged the faithful witness of Antipas, also to death. Antipas is probably to be regarded as a representative of many who had or who would suffer death by refusing to deny the name of Jesus in conforming to the State religion. As Jesus had conquered death, so would his faithful witnesses. The ecclesia was commended for not allowing the martyrdom of Antipas to weaken their belief and their faith in Jesus. The tense used, "thou *didst* not deny" (aorist) is said to indicate one particular, possibly short, period when the ecclesia was tested—probably when Antipas was killed—and had remained loyal.

THE LETTERS TO THE SEVEN CHURCHES OF ASIA

Holding fast the name of Jesus and not denying his faith was a major achievement in the city where Satan's throne was. Today we live in a society which worships many idols, not least among them the State which is often regarded as the universal provider. Loyalty to Jesus is often interpreted by those around as disloyalty to the conventions of men. A witness for Jesus today may have to suffer for his or her witness in many ways. Jesus has the same knowledge and understanding of our particular problems and difficulties as he had of his ecclesia in Pergamum. We look for his return but, when the Son of Man comes, shall he find faith on the earth? May God grant that Jesus will then be able to tell us that we also have held fast his name and not denied his faith.

Nevertheless, all was not well in the ecclesia because it tolerated among its members some *"who hold the teaching of Balaam, who taught Balak to put a stumbling block before the sons of Israel, that they might eat food sacrificed to idols and practise immorality"*. What martyrdom had failed to do, toleration, compromise, was threatening to achieve.

To understand the reference to Balaam, we must go back to early Israelitish history. After the exodus of Israel from Egypt, a covenant was made between God and Israel: *"Now therefore, if you will obey my voice and keep my covenant, you shall be my own possession among all peoples . . . and you shall be to me a kingdom of priests and a holy nation . . . And all the people answered together and said, All that the Lord hath spoken we will do"* (Exodus 19:5,6,8). This covenant was later ratified when Moses sprinkled the blood of oxen on the people after Israel had re-affirmed its pledge of loyalty to God (Exodus 24:7,8). Israel thus became *"a people holy to the LORD your God; the LORD your God has chosen you to be a people for his own possession, out of all the peoples that are on the face of the earth"* (Deuteronomy 7:6). Israel was thus separated to God, which is what holy means. They now belonged to God and as a result were separated from the other nations. This separation from the other nations was not an end in itself but the consequence of Israel becoming God's people. The separation was moral and spiritual rather than physical because Israel remained a nation among the other nations.

THE LETTER TO PERGAMOS

The Old Testament makes it abundantly clear that God's people had been called to show in their lives, individual and national, the moral attributes of their God, revealed to them by His mighty works on their behalf and by lawgiver and prophet. Thus, immediately after the covenant was made, Israel was instructed not to have any gods other than Yahweh, nor bow down to any graven image; and there followed a list of moral qualities which God's people were required to manifest (Exodus 20; cf. Deuteronomy 6:14; 7:1-6,25-26; 13:1-5; 16:16-21).

Apostasy at Baal-Peor

We now go forward to the end of the wilderness journey when Israel was preparing to enter Canaan. Moab and Midian were in Israel's line of advance and Balak, the King of Moab, was so fearful that he asked Balaam to come to him and curse Israel. Balaam came but was impelled by God to bless Israel. Immediately after, the record says: *"While Israel dwelt in Shittim the people began to play the harlot with the daughters of Moab. These invited the people to the sacrifices of their gods, and the people ate, and bowed down to their gods. So Israel yoked himself to Baal of Peor. And the anger of the LORD was kindled against Israel, and the LORD said to Moses, Take all the chiefs of the people, and hang them in the sun before the LORD, that the fierce anger of the LORD may turn away from Israel. And Moses said to the judges of Israel, Every one of you slay his men who have yoked themselves to Baal of Peor"* (Numbers 25:1-5).

The cause of this apostasy is not explained until six chapters later when Moses said that the women *"caused the people of Israel, by the counsel of Balaam, to act treacherously against the LORD in the matter of Peor"* (Numbers 31:16). Balaam, a prophet acknowledging God's control, forbidden by God to curse Israel, so *"loved gain from wrongdoing"* (2 Peter 2:15; cf. Jude 11) that he advised Balak how to achieve the end he so greatly desired (cf. Micah 6:5). The religion of Canaan was extremely licentious and, as in Asia in John's time, there were many temple prostitutes whose services were available to the idol worshippers. The words of Numbers 25 suggest that the seduction of the men of Israel began with the allurements of the temple prostitutes, who then beguiled them into the worship of their gods. Israel's separation to God was threatened both by this worship and the accompanying licentiousness. This was *"the teaching of Balaam"*, who knew that Israel could not continue to be God's people if they behaved in this way. His advice was diabolically clever and could have succeeded had not drastic action been taken against the wrongdoers.

It is significant that immediately after the episode of Peor, Moses repeatedly emphasised in his addresses to Israel that they were a people for God's own possession and His alone (e.g. Deuteronomy 4:20; 7:6; 14:2; 26:18), but the allurements of paganism, the teaching of Balaam, continued to trouble Israel for centuries. Thus, the Books of Kings refer to cult prostitutes, male and female, as part of the evil in Israel (e.g. 1 Kings 14:24; 22:46; 2 Kings 23:7). The appeal to join in the society of their heathen neighbours and share the worship of their gods was a constant temptation to Israel.

The Israel of God

We now come forward to the Christian era. Israel had failed to be a holy nation and this calling was given to a new creation, the true Israel of God. There is a close parallel between the calls of natural and spiritual Israel. Believing men and women, Jew and Gentile alike, had been called to be a people separated to and belonging to God. They had accepted the divine call, saying in effect, as Israel had, All that the Lord hath spoken we will do and we will be obedient. The covenant between God and the new Israel was also sealed by the sprinkling of blood, this time the blood of Jesus (cf. 1 Peter 1:2; for a more detailed exposition, see *The Christadelphian*, 1957, p. 5). And so Peter thought of the duties and privileges of natural Israel as transferred to the Israel of God. He applied the words spoken in Leviticus 11:45 of Israel—*"Ye shall therefore be holy, for I am holy"*—to the new Israel (1 Peter 1:16). He enlarged on this in his second chapter where he applied the words used of natural Israel to the new Israel and made clear the purpose of God's new call: *"You are a chosen race, a royal priesthood, a holy nation, God's own people* (R.V., "a people for God's own possession"), *that you may declare the wonderful deeds of him who*

THE LETTER TO PERGAMOS

called you out of darkness into his marvellous light. Once you were no people but now you are God's people" (1 Peter 2:9-10). Phillips includes in his translation, interpreting rather than translating but catching the apostle's meaning, *"all the old titles of God's people now belong to you"*. He continues, *"It is for you now to demonstrate the goodness of him who has called you"*. The purpose for which God called natural Israel was to be realised by the new Israel of God.

Separation to God

In the opening verse of his first letter (and in 2:11) the apostle Peter called this new Israel "exiles", "sojourners". The same Greek word is used of the patriarchs and denotes persons temporarily resident in a district, people who do not belong to the society in which they live, but who have a higher allegiance elsewhere. They were separated to God and therefore separated from the society, the communal life they had once shared.

Those separated to God could not be other than sojourners in the earth now. One writer expressed it thus: "Scattered over the whole earth, as alien residents of lands in which they could never truly be at home, they were united in a common bond of loyalty to an unseen State of which they sought to prove themselves worthy citizens" (Beare, *The First Epistle of Peter*, p. 49). Such had perforce to continue to live in the world but they were not of it.

This teaching was not unique to Peter. Paul emphasised that believers must not be unequally yoked (mismated, R.S.V.) with unbelievers. They must come out from these, be separate and touch nothing unclean. Christians must do nothing to jeopardise their separation to God and must not compromise with anything in society which is alien to God. They must cleanse themselves from every defilement of body and spirit. This was, or ought to have been, the position of believers in Pergamum but there was a minority in the ecclesia who, by their words and actions, were doing what Balaam had done, weakening or destroying their own separation to God and that of some of their brethren and sisters also, by teaching them to eat food sacrificed to idols and to commit immorality.

THE LETTERS TO THE SEVEN CHURCHES OF ASIA

The appeal of the Balaamites would be primarily to Gentile converts because most, if not all of the Jewish believers would abhor the eating of food sacrificed to idols. The Gentile converts had come out of the society in which they lived to become God's people. It was extremely difficult for them to avoid the contamination of the pagan world to which they had once belonged and in which they had still to live. They were surrounded by activities which appealed to their senses and the only safe course was complete separation from such a society. Their one-time friends were surprised that the converts *"do not now join in the same wild profligacy, and they abuse you"* (1 Peter 4:4). But separation created other and more serious problems. The Lord referred to eating idol sacrifices and committing fornication, the same faults that had occurred at Peor. We must try to understand his language in the light of the customs of that time.

Paganism and Society

There were many societies or social clubs in Pergamum as in the other major cities of Asia Minor. Each society had its own titular deity and met in his temple. A condition of membership of a society was worship in the god's temple. A person wishing to extend hospitality to friends would normally do so in a temple just as today he would use a hotel or restaurant. A little wine was spilled on the floor, with a brief mechanical prayer, as a libation to the god. Or he might invite them to a feast of thanksgiving to a god for a favour rendered. The meat served at the meal would be the remains of an animal offered in sacrifice to the idol. Only a little of the meat was so used; the remainder was the perquisite of the priests and that surplus to their requirements was used for feasts in the temple or sold in the meat market. The thanksgiving to the god was followed by feasting and drinking which usually ended in debauchery. The whole atmosphere was at variance with Christian morality. As already stated, the temples had prostitutes who were at the service of worshippers, who regarded fornication merely a sensual pleasure of no importance. A host might arrange for temple prostitutes to be available to his guests as part of the evening's entertainment and it would be impolite to refuse.

THE LETTER TO PERGAMOS

The whole society in which the believers lived was associated in some way with paganism. Sir William Ramsay has written that these societies, or social clubs, were one of the most deep-rooted customs of Graeco-Roman society which bound their members closely together and represented in its strongest form the pagan spirit in society: "To hold aloof from the clubs was to set oneself down as a mean-spirited, grudging ... person ... devoid of generous impulse and kindly neighbourly feeling, an enemy of mankind" (*The Letters to the Seven Churches,* p. 348). Belonging to such a club or attending a banquet necessarily involved, at the very least, tolerating pagan worship.

The Balaamites rejected the need for absolute separation from such a society. They argued, as some in Corinth had a generation earlier, that an idol had no real existence and therefore a Christian's presence in its temple, even if he performed a formal act of worship, did not mean that he accepted the idol as a real god, even if his pagan host saw that as an act of compromise. And how could something that had no real existence make the flesh of an animal offered to it in sacrifice unfit for eating? They disregarded the restrictions placed on Gentile believers by the apostolic council (Acts 15:20,29) and ignored Paul's warning that they could not *"drink the cup of the Lord and the cup of demons"* nor *"partake of the table of the Lord and the table of demons"* (1 Corinthians 10:21). They ought to have acted so that whether they ate or drank, they did all to the glory of God (10:31). This required them to *"shun the worship of idols"* (10:14). But this was not the only criterion by which they should have judged their actions. The liberty they claimed could *"become a stumbling block to the weak"*, causing them to be destroyed (1 Corinthians 8:9-11). And so Paul wrote that if food caused his brother to stumble, he would refrain from eating meat.

The Things of this World

The Balaamites ignored Paul's words. To them an idol's temple was no more than an eating place, and meat offered in sacrifice was still only meat and could be eaten by believers. The real reason for their attitude was that refusal to eat meat sacrificed to idols would have involved their exclusion from all the societies, from society in general, and they were not prepared to make such a sacrifice. They wanted to compromise, to get out into and enjoy the society around them and probably justified this by saying that, so doing, they would be able to influence it and remove misunderstandings about Christians. The Balaamites would not forego practices which might cause their brethren and sisters to stumble. On the contrary, they encouraged these to go to idol temples, knowing full well that believers in an idol's temple would be tempted as Israel had been at Peor and could easily revert to actions they had once regarded as normal by committing fornication. Chastity before and fidelity in marriage were virtually unique then to Christianity and very hard for converts to achieve who had been used to promiscuity. The Balaamites were ready to place themselves and their brethren and sisters in situations which would compromise their belief in the one God and the manner of life He required of His people. Like Balaam, they loved the wages of unrighteousness, the pleasures society could offer, although these would destroy their separation to God.

The Believer's Separation

The Lord's command to the ecclesia to refrain from eating food sacrificed to idols could only be expressed in the language of that time but looking behind that language to the principle involved we find this required complete separation of believers from the manner of life of the society in which they lived. Each succeeding generation of believers has had to work out what the Lord's command required of them. We are exposed to the seductions of a world very similar to that at Pergamum and we too can be tempted to compromise with the society in which we live, join in its activities and accept its customs.

There are many institutes, clubs and so on in the world in which we live. Can we join these? For example, ought a brother to become a freemason? One wishing to do so could say that the religious aspect of freemasonry is so much mumbo jumbo which no-one takes seriously. But he should ask himself if his wish to join such a society is basically a desire to enter part of the social

THE LETTER TO PERGAMOS

life around him from which he would otherwise be excluded. This applies to all the other clubs, institutes and the like. We sometimes hear brethren and sisters ask what is the harm in what they propose to do. The question each one of us should ask is not this but, Will what I wish to do strengthen or weaken my separation, or that of my brethren and sisters to God? We must be absolutely honest with ourselves and reject whatever would weaken our separation to God. This test of our actions will show that very few, if any, of the activities in society around us will, if we join them, increase our separation to God. On the contrary, they could well be traps on the path to the Kingdom of God which could cause us, or some of our brethren and sisters, to stumble and fall. We must never by a careless manner of life, by seeking what pleases us rather than the things that build up others, allow ourselves to be placed in positions incompatible with our faith or its moral standards. It is easy to allow a desire, perhaps subconscious, for participation in the activities of society around us to cause us to compromise with it, using specious arguments such as influencing society for good, commending our religion to it and showing that really we are nice people. The joys of the age to come expressed in the rewards promised to the ecclesias are so wonderful that it would be foolish indeed to allow the pleasures of society around us to weaken our separation to God and thus jeopardise our hope of the future. We must not follow the teaching of Balaam which could easily lead us also to commit fornication.

The World's Standards

It is not pleasant to talk of this possibility but we must not shut our eyes to the nature of society around us. There has been a revolution in recent years regarding sexual ethics. The sex education now given in schools is "based on the premise that sexual intimacy at any age is a physical activity on a par with football or hockey" (*The Daily Telegraph*, 29.9.80). And so the contraceptive pill has been given by doctors to girls under 16 without their parents' knowledge or even against their parents' wishes. Despite the use of the pill, illegitimacy rates in England and Scotland—10% of all live births—are at their highest ever.

THE LETTERS TO THE SEVEN CHURCHES OF ASIA

A sex manual for teenagers widely used in schools regards sexual activities roundly condemned in Scripture as not uncommon nor even abnormal. Such activities are encouraged by sex shops now operating in many towns which sell pornographic books and films. Against such a background, one is not surprised to read in the annual reports of the Universities and Colleges Christian Fellowship for 1979 and 1980 that the student community is widely immoral and that 70% of all women students at Oxford are sexually experienced by their third year. Similar figures obtain in other universities and among young girls in France, Italy, the United States of America and South Africa as well as Great Britain. Young girls solicit the favours of elderly men; husbands and wives who become bored with or indifferent to one another in middle age can obtain divorce by consent. Almost one-third of marriages in England now end in divorce and the figure is appreciably higher in the United States.

Sexual permissiveness is encouraged by scenes shown on T.V. and in cinemas. We are told of the possibility that unregulated and uncontrollable T.V. from satellites will enter our homes. These programmes might include "something not far off pornography". This prospect is frightening. Add to these influences the bad language, blasphemy and smutty jokes of many of those among whom some of us have to work and it will be seen that the influence of society around us is inimical to the believer.

Many in the churches around us are trying to come to terms with the new morality by adapting Christian sexual ethics to it. Christian thinking on sexual morality is said to need fundamental reconstruction, as illustrated by a continuing debate in the churches on homosexuality. The Oxford University Graduate Chaplain wrote recently that "a massive attempt is going on within the churches to change the entire basis of sexual ethics for Christians".

The sexual impulse is one of the strongest in men and women but the Christian controls it by chastity before marriage and lifelong fidelity to the other partner in marriage, in which the husband, in his love for his wife, mirrors Christ's love for his church.

THE LETTER TO PERGAMOS

Sex is not an activity on a par with eating and drinking but an expression of love by which husband and wife become one flesh. The Song of Songs shows the joy husband and wife can and should have in each other. The society around us is startlingly similar to that in Pergamum 1900 years ago in rejecting this and adopting a casual attitude to sex. We may find it as difficult as some in Pergamum to resist the pressure to conform to the usages of those around us, or we may be tempted to adapt Christian ethics to what we think they will accept. The Word of God must determine our standards and not society around us. The main danger to us, as to those in Pergamum, may come from teaching which purports to be Christian, as Balaam's advice came from one who was nominally a prophet.

A great responsibility rests on us, as on our brethren and sisters at Pergamum. We are not told to go out of the world (1 Corinthians 5:10) but to manifest in our lives in it the Christian standards laid down in the New Testament. Those of us who have children have the great responsibility of ensuring that they are adequately prepared to face the seductions of society around them. Each one of us must ensure that we do not diminish our witness by thoughtless words or actions. There can be no compromise between the Christian's standards and those of the world around him. Each one of us needs reminding that we are not our own, but God's possession bought at a great price, the precious blood of Christ. We have become God's people to show in our lives the excellencies, the virtues of the God who called us from darkness, and to be holy in all our conduct as He who called us is holy. We can only do this if we are separated to Him and reject whatever would weaken this separation.

The Teaching of the Nicolaitans

The Lord continued: *"So you also have some who hold the teaching of the Nicolaitans."* ("So" = *houtō*, in this fashion, i.e. that of the Balaamites in the preceding verse.) The Nicolaitans are mentioned in Scripture only here and in the letter to Ephesus and nothing is known for certain about them. If a writer almost a century later is to be trusted (Iranaeus, A.D. 182-8) the Nicolaitans took their name from Nicolaus, one of the seven (Acts 6:5), and whose teaching they perverted. They taught that the body was of no importance and therefore regarded sensual sins with indifference because the spirit was uncontaminated by them. They were probably people who, using Paul's phrase, felt able to continue in sin that grace might abound but who in reality perverted the grace of God into licentiousness. The effect of their teaching was thus essentially similar to that of the Balaamites. This is supported by the Lord's words which in the Greek almost certainly indicate that the teaching of the Nicolaitans and its outcome were identical with those of the Balaamites, but the Nicolaitans may have been even more tolerant of sexual immorality.

The Nicolaitans were active in Ephesus and Pergamum, the commercial and official capitals of the province where they would especially feel the need for accommodation with society. They, like the Balaamites, would doubtless argue that, far from destroying the faith, they were trying to effect an acceptable compromise with the customs of the Graeco-Roman world and thus make it appeal to those around them: 'It will put up with some of your beliefs if you will accept some of its customs; there is need for give and take on both sides.'

They forgot that a compromise between Christianity and paganism was unacceptable to our Lord. He, through John, saw both the Balaamites and Nicolaitans as in reality what, during the war years, would have been called fifth columnists. The compromise they offered presented an even greater danger to the ecclesia than paganism or emperor worship. These were open opponents which the ecclesia was successfully resisting, whereas the others were insidious dangers within the ecclesia, which was in danger of losing all it had achieved by its fidelity to Jesus when it allowed such teachers a place in the ecclesia. Nicolaitan teaching, like that of the Balaamites, is constantly re-appearing but the lesson of Pergamum is that believers must not attempt to combine ways of life which do not belong together.

Our predecessors a century ago were often ostracised for their faith. There was then little temptation to effect a compromise

THE LETTER TO PERGAMOS

between the Truth and the society in which they lived. Today, the churches around us seek to make their beliefs acceptable to society and so they are ready, as we have said, to tolerate practices condemned in Scripture. We can be affected by such an attitude. The ancient heresy that a Christian can mix with a society such as that in which we live and yet continue to be a genuine Christian is not unknown among us. The standards of the Truth are as different today from those of society as they were at Pergamum. We may be truly Biblical in our beliefs but this is valueless if it does not result in purity of conduct. Our Lord in this letter reinforced the teaching of other parts of the New Testament by insisting that holy living can only be achieved by a separation from such a society.

The contrast with the position at Ephesus is marked. There the works of the Nicolaitans were hated but at Pergamum they were tolerated. We do not know the cause of this toleration. The teachers of evil may have been prominent members of the ecclesia or they may have been reluctant to withdraw fellowship from members for any cause.

A Lack of Leadership

Whatever the reason for toleration, there had obviously been a lack of leadership in the ecclesia, the members of which should have been told that such evil teachers could not be allowed to remain in the ecclesia. This mistaken leniency was endangering the ecclesia and hence the command to the brethren and sisters who had not embraced the erroneous teaching was clear and unequivocal. *"Repent then"*—literally *"Repent thou therefore"* (Marshall); cease as an ecclesia to tolerate these teachers as Ephesus had done. The ecclesia had the example of Israel at Peor, where drastic action was needed to avert God's anger. If the ecclesia failed to act, Jesus would come to the ecclesia quickly. The words *"I will come to you"* are the same as those to Ephesus in verse 5 but here *"quickly"* is added. The resolution of the problem brooked no delay. Jesus would come quickly to the ecclesia and war against the evil teachers with the sword of his mouth.

THE LETTERS TO THE SEVEN CHURCHES OF ASIA

A distinction is made between those in the ecclesia who tolerated the evil teaching although they did not endorse it and the minority who accepted it. The Lord's coming under such circumstances could not be other than unpleasant to the ecclesia but the sword of judgement in his mouth would be used only against the evil-doers. We do not know how the Lord would war against them. As with Jezebel and her followers in Thyatira, it may have been physical calamity, sickness or sudden death but, whatever the means, the ecclesia would know that the Lord had come in judgement.

The different reactions to the Nicolaitans at Ephesus and Pergamum show how difficult it was then to combine ecclesial discipline with love and understanding and the same is true today. But it is the ideal which we must strive to attain.

6

THE LETTER TO THYATIRA

THE road from Pergamum to Sardis and Laodicea which connected the valleys of the Caikos and Hermus rivers, went through the fertile valley of the river Lycus which flows southwest to join the Hermus. Much of the trade between these rich valleys went along this road. Thyatira was situated a little off this road, about half-way between Pergamum and Sardis, but the city was connected by a direct route to Philadelphia. It had been built about 300 B.C. by Seleucus I as a garrison town, to act as a defensive outpost for his kingdom which extended from the Hermus valley eastward to the Euphrates. Thyatira lacked natural defences; fortifications had therefore to be built and the town garrisoned with reliable Macedonian soldiers.

Seleucus I favoured the Jews and made them citizens of the cities he founded in his kingdom and it is therefore very probable that he settled Jews in Thyatira. Judaism apart, Thyatiran religion was basically similar to that of the other cities. The Macedonian soldiers brought their own gods with them and combined their worship with that of the gods they found in the city. 30 years before John wrote, Thyatira ceased to be merely a military city and began to increase in size, and commercial importance. This accelerated during the next century, but in John's time, Thyatira was still a relatively small city.

"A seller of purple"

Close links were maintained between Thyatira—and other cities which contained Macedonian colonies—and the homeland in Macedonia. Paul's first convert in Philippi, Lydia, a seller of purple (dye) was probably on a business trip from Thyatira. Purple then had a much wider meaning than now. The purple of Thyatira would today be known as turkey red and was made from the root of the madder plant which grew abundantly in this region. (The dye continued to be produced from madder until chemists synthesised it in the last century.) Lydia had probably come into contact with Judaism in Thyatira and, like many others, had been attracted by its monotheism and high moral teaching and had adopted certain Jewish customs, including Sabbath observance at the synagogue, without actually becoming a proselyte (Acts 13:14-16,26; 17:2-4,17; 18:7). We are not told how the Truth was introduced to Thyatira but, if Lydia was on a visit to Philippi, she would bring the Gospel message with her when she returned; otherwise Paul's extended stay in Ephesus, when *"all the residents of Asia heard the word of the Lord, both Jews and Greeks"* is the most likely origin of the ecclesia in Thyatira (Acts 19:10).

A Small Ecclesia

The longest of the seven letters was written to the ecclesia in the smallest and least important of the seven cities. We do not know the size of the Thyatiran ecclesia but it could well be that it too was small. Size, either of an ecclesia or the city in which it is, is no criterion of importance in the Lord's eyes. Here is an encouragement not only to the Thyatiran brethren and sisters but to all those throughout the world today who labour in small ecclesias.

"The words of the Son of God, who has eyes like a flame of fire, and whose feet are like burnished bronze" (Revelation 2:18). This description of the Lord is taken from Revelation 1 except that the apostle's words *"one like a son of man"* are replaced by *"Son of God"*; this phrase occurs nowhere else in the whole book. There are references in the letter to Psalm 2 (v. 26—Psalm 2:8; v. 27—Psalm 2:9) in which the Lord's anointed is called God's Son (Psalm 2:7). The title Son of God could stem from the use of this psalm by Jesus but I suggest the Lord employed it primarily to emphasise to a small ecclesia his unique status, his power and authority. The believers were related to the Son of God who would sustain them if they held fast, but could also inflict punishment on unrepentant evildoers in the ecclesia.

THE LETTER TO THYATIRA

"Who has eyes like a flame of fire" means the same as when the Lord described himself to Pergamum as having the sharp two-edged sword. All things were open and laid bare to the eyes of him with whom they had to do. His discernment was so keen that nothing concerning an individual member or the ecclesia as a whole was hidden from the Lord. The eyes of Jesus are the physical feature which most impressed the Gospel writers. He looked with anger on the Pharisees (Mark 3:5) but with love on the rich young man (Mark 10:21). He looked up at Zacchaeus and the chief tax collector came down joyfully from the tree to receive his self-invited guest (Luke 19:1-7). He turned and looked on Peter, and the apostle who had just denied him went out and wept bitterly (Luke 22:61-62). Those features were preserved in the risen Lord. His eyes could convey love and understanding or flash with anger. Here was both comfort and warning to them and to us. He knows and understands not only our needs, difficulties and problems but also those innermost thoughts and actions which we may hide from one another.

Treading Out in Judgement

"Whose feet are like burnished bronze". The Greek word translated "burnished bronze" occurs only here and in Revelation 1:15. Burnished bronze was a very hard alloy which may have been a unique product of the Thyatiran bronze-workers and thus having a meaning for them which escapes us today. A later chapter (Revelation 19:15) tells of the day when the Lord will tread the wine press of the fury of the wrath of God the Almighty. Feet made of burnished bronze are well equipped for this task but the use of this figure in this letter reminded the brethren and sisters that judgement was not restricted to that great day but would be inflicted on evil-doers in the ecclesia if they did not repent. We shall see later what the judgement involved.

"I know your works, your love and faith and service and patient endurance, and that your latter works exceed the first." The One with eyes like a flame of fire had looked at the ecclesia and found much in it to praise. His verdict could not be challenged and would bring joy to the brethren and sisters. If Lydia had introduced the

THE LETTERS TO THE SEVEN CHURCHES OF ASIA

Truth to Thyatira, her influence had been very beneficial. This illustrates the great effect a sister of Christlike character can have in an ecclesia.

The Lord's words are reminiscent of Paul's praise of the Thessalonians (1 Thessalonians 1:3; 2 Thessalonians 1:3) and of his own commendation of the Ephesian ecclesia (Revelation 2:2-3) but there was an all-important difference. The brethren and sisters at Ephesus no longer loved as they had at first whereas the love of those in Thyatira, far from diminishing, had increased with the years. Like the Hebrews, the Thyatiran ecclesia showed their love for God in serving the saints (Hebrews 6:10). Their faith worked through love (Galatians 5:6) and led to the patient endurance of all their difficulties.

So it must be with us today. Love for God and Jesus, if it is to be real, must express itself in service which increases as we mature in the Truth. How often the Lord's parables emphasise that he expects active service from his followers while he is absent. And we too must show the patient endurance which is the outcome of faith, of absolute trust in God and Jesus and their promises. *"By faith he (Moses) left Egypt, not being afraid of the anger of the king, for he endured as seeing him who is invisible"* (Hebrews 11:27). We need a like faith if we are to hold fast the confession of our faith without wavering in these difficult days and the more trying ones still to come; this faith comes only from the Word of God.

We embrace the Truth with fervour and no labour for it is too great, but the years can dampen this enthusiasm and our works decrease. Our love grows cold, service becomes burdensome, faith weakens and patient endurance flags. How happy the ecclesia to which we belong will be if the Lord is able to tell us that these qualities had increased until his coming, that we had not relaxed our efforts but were working with ever-increasing diligence to minister the Word to, and to serve, one another. It rests with every member of an ecclesia, not just with those elected to office, if the Lord at his coming will be able to commend us as he did the Thyatiran ecclesia.

One might have expected that such praise indicated that Thyatira was a model ecclesia; this was not so: *"But I have this*

THE LETTER TO THYATIRA

against you, that you tolerate the woman Jezebel, who calls herself a prophetess and is teaching and beguiling my servants to practise immorality and to eat food sacrificed to idols.'' The danger came from a prominent sister within the ecclesia. At Ephesus, the need for sound teaching had been emphasised in such a way that love had been lost, whereas love was shown at Thyatira but ecclesial discipline had not been maintained, with the result that serious error was tolerated. Each ecclesia was weak where the other was strong, showing—as we saw under Pergamum—how difficult it is to combine love and the maintenance of sound teaching. As Brother John Thomas put it, love is long suffering but it can be too long suffering, too tolerant. Those who called themselves apostles had not been tested and rejected as at Ephesus.

Today we have to try to hold the right balance between action to preserve the deposit entrusted to us and manifesting love in our ecclesial life. We live in a permissive age when most things "go". This may influence us either to tolerate what ought not to be permitted in an ecclesia or to be too harsh in our judgements. Neither attitude is acceptable to our Lord and we must try to steer a course between these extremes, however difficult this may be.

In Pergamum some members held the teaching of Balaam and were breaking down the separation of their brethren and sisters to God, just as Balaam had done centuries earlier with Israel. The Lord's choice of the name Jezebel to denote the erring sister at Thyatira must likewise indicate that her actions were in principle similar to those of Queen Jezebel. During the reigns of Omri and Ahab the Kingdom of Israel was badly in need of allies and found one in Ethbaal, King of the Sidonians, said by Josephus to be also "the priest of Astarte" (*Against Apion*, Book 1, para. 18).

Phoenicia was becoming a wealthy power, with fleets which traded as far west as Great Britain and as far east as India. The country provided a market for Israel's produce and the alliance was thus advantageous to Israel commercially as well as politically. It was sealed by the marriage of Ahab to Jezebel, Ethbaal's daughter. A princess marrying into a foreign country had the right for herself and her retinue to worship their own gods in her new country. This had earlier been conceded by Solomon to the foreign princesses he married and the King had built high places for the worship of their gods, in which he himself joined (1 Kings 11:1-8).

Halting Between Two Opinions

Ahab had placed himself in a position where he was unable to restrain Jezebel's idolatrous practices, even if he had wished to do so. Rather, for these same reasons and following Solomon's example, Ahab erected an altar in the house of Baal which he built in Samaria and himself worshipped Baal. Again like Solomon, Ahab did not wish to abandon the worship of Yahweh. The names of the three of his children preserved in the Old Testament each incorporated part of the Divine Name and were meant to honour Yahweh. Ahab still consulted a prophet of Yahweh (1 Kings 22:5-8, 15-17) but he wished to worship both Yahweh and Baal. The King's influence ensured that the majority of his people followed his example. They would realise that renunciation of Baal must endanger the alliance with Ethbaal and result in a fall in their standard of living, and so only 7,000 in Israel had not bowed the knee to Baal. Acceptance of Baal involved participation in the immorality associated with his worship.

There were other gods besides Baal in the Canaanite Phoenician pantheon of gods and Jezebel would worship Astarte, of whom her father was a priest, and other gods. She would have been content with the worship of Baal in Israel alongside that of Yahweh, perhaps hoping that in time Baal would be acknowledged as overlord; but there was a minority in Israel which refused to do this. The 7,000 dissenters were led by the prophets of the Lord, particularly Elijah. This great prophet put the issue with stark clarity in his confrontation with the prophets of Baal on Mount Carmel, asking the people how long they would *"go limping with two different opinions? If the Lord is God, follow him; but if Baal, then follow him"* (1 Kings 18:21). In Elijah's view there was no place in Israel for the worship of gods other than Yahweh. This uncompromising attitude, so unlike the "civilised code" of tolerating the gods of other nations, infuriated Jezebel and led her to try to exterminate this obstinate minority. The difference

THE LETTER TO THYATIRA

between Jezebel and Elijah was crystal clear. Was Yahweh the only god or one among many? The Queen regarded Yahweh as one among many and refused to acknowledge that He alone was God.

Looking in more detail at the situation in Thyatira we see how apt was the Lord's choice of the name Jezebel to denote the activities of the sister there. Thyatira was a Macedonian colony. In Macedonia women held an honoured and influential position exceptional in the ancient world (cf. the two sisters at Philippi who had quarrelled) and it is consistent with this to find a sister playing a prominent part in the Thyatiran ecclesia.

Trade Guilds

The societies or social clubs in Thyatira had an added function that greatly increased their importance. They were trade guilds which looked after the professional interests of their members and more of these are known to have existed in Thyatira than in any other of the seven cities. Woolworkers, dyers, potters, bronze smiths etc. belonged to separate guilds. A craftsman in one of these occupations would find it extremely difficult, if not impossible, to follow his trade unless he or she was a member of the appropriate guild, which also acted as a kind of mutual benefit society, helping its members if they fell on hard times. Each guild met in the temple of its titular deity where it worshipped that deity, even if only perfunctorily. These guilds "bound their members closely together in virtue of the common sacrificial meal, a scene of enjoyment following a religious ceremony . . . Such revels were not merely condoned by pagan opinion but were regarded as a duty, in which graver natures ought occasionally to relax their seriousness, and yield to the impulses of nature, in order to return again with fresh zest to the real work of life" (Ramsay, *The Letters to the Seven Churches*, pp. 348,349). Some Gentile converts would have been members of one of these guilds before their baptism. What ought their subsequent attitude to be? Ought they to continue as members of a guild, paying their subscription to it, or leave it, thus condemning themselves and their families to poverty?

The problem these Thyatiran believers faced must not be

under-estimated but it was part of a larger problem, the relationship of the ecclesia to the society in which it lived. Ought the ecclesia to adapt to the customs around it? This was essentially the same problem as at Pergamum but whereas there the basic problem was a reluctance to forego the pleasures of social life, at Thyatira it was economic. This made it possible to argue more plausibly that an accommodation with the society in which they lived was more sensible than an attitude which must ultimately result in a collision with it. Thus Jezebel was *"teaching and beguiling my servants to practise immorality and to eat food sacrificed to idols"*. The implication of the Lord's words is clear: Jezebel considered it unreasonable to expect a convert to withdraw from a guild, thus losing all hope of benefit and dissociating himself from those objectives of the guild which were praiseworthy and beneficial. What possible harm could there be in combining membership of a guild with that of the ecclesia? Surely it could not be wrong to be a member of a guild which protected their interests and helped in times of sickness or misfortune! The convert would suffer a considerable financial loss if he left the guild, just as abandonment of Baal worship in Israel would have reduced the nation's standard of living. He could not be expected to accept this. The revels at guild meetings often led to fornication but this was unimportant. As at Pergamum, those with "knowledge" thought that immorality affected the body only and left the spirit untouched. One must expect believers who went to a guild feast to behave like their pagan companions but this did no harm to them.

Jezebel's Teaching

Jezebel thus taught the Lord's servants to practise immorality and verse 23 suggests that she herself did so. A believer could remain a member of a guild, honour the god in whose temple the guild meeting was held and join in what went on there. He should acknowledge the gods around him in their appropriate spheres. Jezebel did not intend to reject Christianity but regarded it as one only of the religions of the Roman empire and Jesus as one of many lords. Jesus would be acknowledged together with the emperor and the pagan deities as a member of the pantheon of gods, each with his or her appropriate sphere, just as Emperor

THE LETTER TO THYATIRA

Severus proposed more than a century later. The effect of Jezebel's teaching was thus in principle identical with what Queen Jezebel had tried to do in Israel. Her claim to be a prophetess, perhaps supported by some kind of "sign", was made to add authority to her teaching, enabling her to claim a new revelation and set aside earlier apostolic instructions. The compromise she proposed would have been fatal to true Christianity just as Queen Jezebel's action if successful would ultimately have destroyed the worship of Yahweh.

Some well-known later converts from paganism (Justin Martyr, Ignatius and Clement of Alexandria) found in paganism religious truths which prepared the way for the Christian faith, while condemning the moral evils associated with paganism. Apologists in the century after John, writing in defence of Christianity, appealed for toleration by non-Christians because there was little difference between Christianity and the teaching of the best Greek philosophers (Iranaeus A.D. 182-8, Hippolytus about A.D. 225, Clement of Alexandria a little earlier than Hippolytus).

The ecclesia at Thyatira, if it failed to persuade Jezebel to change her teaching, ought to have withdrawn fellowship from her. Instead, it had tolerated Jezebel, "let her alone" as the word can mean (e.g. Matthew 15:14; Mark 14:6; Luke 13:8; John 12:7; Acts 5:38), to continue her teaching in the ecclesia, and by this toleration incurred a terrible responsibility. (The word translated "tolerate", *aphiēmi*, is a more emphatic word than "have" in v. 15.) The enormity of the offence is emphasised by the use of the possessive pronoun "my" (*emos*), meaning "what belongs to me", the only time this possessive pronoun is used in the whole book.

Jezebel was beguiling those who belonged to Jesus. Why had ecclesial action not been taken against her? She was a member of an ecclesia praised for its service and was therefore presumably what today would be called a sister of "good works". Further, earlier scholars (Alford, Wordsworth etc.) accepted an alternative text which read "the woman of thine", i.e. "thy wife Jezebel" for "the woman Jezebel". This is given in the Revised Version margin although modern translators prefer "the woman". If "thy wife" is the correct text, Jezebel, in modern parlance, was the wife of the recording brother or of an arranging brother. However this may be, Jezebel, like her namesake centuries earlier, was an able, energetic, managing woman who also did good works. These qualities made her teaching dangerous but help to explain the reluctance of the angel of the ecclesia to take action against her, whether or not she was married to a prominent brother in the meeting.

Ahab, centuries earlier, had good reasons as a statesman for his alliance with Ethbaal and for his attitude to Queen Jezebel's activities. He was trying to persuade the kingdoms of the area to form an alliance to oppose the rising power of Assyria. This alliance fought a major battle with the Assyrians and halted their advance westward; it was more than a century before they invaded Israel. But the cost of Ahab's success was unfaithfulness to his God.

The angel of the ecclesia could likewise advance good reasons for his toleration of the woman Jezebel. He would argue that people must not be alienated, that the ecclesia would be divided by action against Jezebel and suffer a heavy loss if such an influential sister were expelled. So he permitted her to remain a member of the ecclesia and continue her teaching. Like Ahab, he would regard his attitude as statesmanlike but, again like Ahab, it involved him in unfaithfulness to his God. Failure to restrain Jezebel permitted her to lead astray members of the flock for which he was responsible. The Lord with eyes like a flame of fire saw this and reproved him.

A Duty to be Faced

There is a lesson here for disciples of every age. Brother Roberts wrote: "Withdrawal is a serious step, and ought not to be lightly taken against any brother" (*Ecclesial Guide*, Section 32, p. 24) but if wrong teaching on a first principle of belief or conduct is persisted in, the ecclesia must dissociate itself from the one who teaches error, however prominent he or she may be in the ecclesia. This is a very unpleasant duty but one not to be shirked if the ecclesia is to be faithful to its Lord.

"*I gave her time to repent, but she refuses* (lit. wishes not, willeth not, cf. John 5:40 and 7:17) *to repent of her immorality.*" Despite

THE LETTER TO THYATIRA

Jezebel's heinous teaching, the Lord, not willing that any should perish, had given her time for repentance. Perhaps she had earlier been warned by John when he was resident in Ephesus. The evil had existed for some time but Jezebel ignored the opportunity for repentance—just as had her namesake during the years of drought—and obstinately adhered to her policy of compromise with paganism. *"Because sentence against an evil deed is not executed speedily, the heart of the sons of men is fully set to do evil"* (Ecclesiastes 8:11). And so the passage of time hardened Jezebel's resolve and she refused to repent. God's patience had waited for her as it had in the days of Noah but now judgement would come as it had then (1 Peter 3:20). The ecclesia had not acted against Jezebel but the Lord would.

"Behold, I will throw her on a sickbed, and those who commit adultery with her I will throw into great tribulation, unless they repent of her doings; and I will strike her children dead." "I will throw" is literally, "I am throwing": the tense indicated the imminence of the punishment (cf. John 20:17, "I am ascending" *or* "I am about to ascend"). The word "throw", or "cast" (translated "lay" in verse 24), does not imply that violence will be used but indicates the prostration of sickness. The word here translated "sickbed" (*klinē*) is elsewhere in the New Testament rendered "bed" but it means that on which one lies, a couch or bed, and is used of the couch on which a guest at a banquet reclined. The word could here well have this meaning. Women did not feast publicly with men at guild meetings, unless they were there for entertainment and immorality. This suggests that Jezebel had literally committed adultery and her punishment was that the luxurious couch on which she had sinned would be replaced by a bed of pain. The words are reminiscent of Psalm 41:3-4 which the Lord may have had in mind: *"May the Lord help him upon the bed of his pain; thou hast made all his bed in his sickness. I said, O Lord, have mercy upon me; heal my soul, for I have sinned against thee"* (LXX). Unlike the Psalmist, Jezebel refused to repent but those who committed adultery with her, probably meaning those who had been seduced to commit adultery as she did, rather than commit adultery *with* her, still had an opportunity to repent of *her* doings, or her works.

THE LETTERS TO THE SEVEN CHURCHES OF ASIA

If, like her, they refused, they would be thrown into great tribulation. The choice was between the works of Jezebel which they were doing (verse 22) and the works of Christ which the faithful did (verse 26). Compromise was impossible.

"I will strike her children dead." These children may have been the offspring of her adulteries. David was told that, because by his adultery with Bathsheba, he had utterly scorned the Lord, the child that was born to him would die (2 Samuel 12:14) and, similarly, Jezebel's children would die. (We do not know if the reference in 2 Kings 9:22 to Queen Jezebel's harlotries is to be taken literally, although a worshipper of Baal and Astarte could well not be chaste.) Alternatively, "her children" may refer to Jezebel's spiritual progeny, who endorsed and promulgated her teaching (cf. Isaiah 57:3-5) and therefore were to be condemned more strongly than those in the preceding verse who succumbed to temptation. *"I will strike her children dead"* is literally, *"I will kill her children with death"*. The word translated death (*thanatos*) is often used in the LXX for the Hebrew word translated pestilence in the A.V., R.V., etc. (e.g. Exodus 5:3; Leviticus 26:25; Numbers 14:12; Deuteronomy 28:21; 2 Samuel 24:13,15; 1 Kings 8:37; Psalm 78:50). These children, like those in Jeremiah's time, would *"die of deadly diseases"* (Jeremiah 16:4) and not *"the common death of all men"* (Numbers 16:29). The death of Queen Jezebel's prophets at the brook Kishon was an obvious sign that the Lord alone was God; similarly, the judgement on the woman Jezebel, on those who committed adultery like her, and on her children, would be so startling that *"all the churches shall know that I am he who searches mind and heart, and I will give to each of you as your works deserve"*.

God's Standard

The phrase "each of you" makes the words which follow personal to each member rather than a message just to the "angel" of the ecclesia. Each would be given according to his works. This has always been God's standard of judgement of the believer and will be in the last days. None could by their works earn or in any way deserve eternal life but their works showed if they were of Christ or of Jezebel (Psalm 62:12; Jeremiah 17:10; Matthew

16:27; 1 Peter 1:17). The Lord's words would bring comfort to those unsullied by Jezebel's teaching and works but a fearful warning to others.

We live in days when God does not openly intervene to show His displeasure with persistent offenders. He gives them time to repent but, like Jezebel, they may not be willing to do so, tempted (as she was) to act as if the day of judgement will never come and all things will continue as they were from the beginning of creation. They—may I say, we—may rebel at exclusion from activities of the society around us and forget the day of judgement; but this will surely come, however long it may seem to us to be deferred. *"The Lord will judge his people"* and *"It is a fearful thing to fall into the hands of the living God."*

Let us not throw away our confidence which has a great reward. For we have need of endurance so that we may do the will of God and receive what is promised. For yet a little while, and the coming one shall come and shall not tarry. But we are not of those who shrink back and are destroyed, but of those who have faith and keep their souls (Hebrews 10:30,31,35-39).

"Keep yourselves from idols"

The Lord then addressed words of comfort *"to the rest of you in Thyatira, who do not hold this teaching, who have not learned what some call the deep things of Satan, to you I say, I do not lay upon you any other burden; only hold fast what you have, until I come"*. Jezebel taunted those who rejected her teaching as lacking knowledge of the deep things of the Truth; but the deep things of which she is so proud are not, says the Lord, the deep things of God (1 Corinthians 2:10) but of the adversary. The Lord did not condone their lack of action against Jezebel but, having said that he himself would deal with her, laid upon them no burden additional to that they had already. The phrase is so reminiscent of the words of the apostolic decree (Acts 15:28) that it is clear that the burden the true believer could not escape was abstinence from eating things sacrificed to idols and from fornication. Jezebel had not received a new revelation which superseded the apostolic decree and nothing more was required of true believers than that they keep a firm hold on what they had until the Lord came, continuing in love, faith, service and patient endurance. He who keeps the Lord's works until the end will be given a rich reward.

The people of God in every age have been subject to the temptation to worship idols, and it has never been easy for them to keep themselves from such (1 John 5:21; cf. Acts 15:20). Idols need not be images of metal or stone, graven by art and device of man (Acts 17:29, R.V.). The first century was a materialistic age and the inhabitants of the cities of Asia Minor were interested, first and foremost, in making money and enjoying the comforts and luxuries it provided. These words could equally well describe the society in which we live. An author has written that we are "a people whose religion has become a belief in technology and a life increasingly devoted to a search for an ever-higher material standard of living" (Gaster, *A Morning without Clouds*. Quoted in review by J. A. B. Peel in *The Daily Telegraph*, 3.9.81).

Paul, in the materialistic first century, wrote to ecclesias in Asia Minor in very blunt terms: *"Be sure of this, that no immoral or impure man, or one who is covetous (that is, an idolater), has any inheritance in the kingdom of Christ and of God. Let no one deceive you with empty words, for it is because of these things that the wrath of God comes upon the sons of disobedience. Therefore do not associate with them"* (Ephesians 5:5-7). The covetous man is an idolater and, like the immoral person, has no place in God's Kingdom. The believer is instructed to keep his life free from the love of money. Again, *"Put to death what is earthly in you: immorality, impurity, passion, evil desire, and covetousness, which is idolatry. On account of these the wrath of God is coming. In these you once walked, when you lived in them. But now put them all away"* (Colossians 3:5-8). Here too covetousness is equated with idolatry and included in the evil works the believer has to put to death. Covetousness was included among *"all manner of wickedness"* in which Gentiles indulged (Romans 1:29). In all these citations Paul was reiterating the words of the Lord and, indeed, of the Law (Exodus 20:17). Jesus included coveting among the evil things which came from the heart of man (Mark 7:22; cf. Luke 12:15). The word translated "covetousness" (*pleonexia*) is also rendered greed and means grasping greed and possessiveness.

THE LETTER TO THYATIRA

We, like these early believers, need reminding of the Lord's words: *"No man can serve two masters; for either he will hate the one and love the other, or he will be devoted to the one and despise the other. You cannot serve God and mammon"* (Matthew 6:24). Our allegiance is to God or to mammon. The covetous man is condemned so severely because he has an object of worship other than God; he is repeating the error of Jezebel. We may think this is a mistake we shall never make but there are many things, even persons, which can usurp the place God alone should have in our lives. These include ambition, the desire for money, for keeping up with the Jones' as they acquire more expensive cars, the latest in home entertainment, our hobbies, and so on. There is no harm in improving the conditions under which we live, in obtaining higher education and the like but when we put these things and the means to attain them first in our lives, and give priority to them over our service to God, we are idolaters, seeking to worship more than one God. Those who have least in this life can be the most covetous. Let us keep a correct sense of proportion in our activities in life and, as we increase our knowledge or resources, use them in the service of God.

> Jesus calls us from the worship
> Of the vain world's golden store,
> From each idol that would keep us,
> Saying, "Christian, love me more".

And so we pray:

> Is there a thing beneath the sun
> That strives with Thee my heart to share?
> Ah, tear it thence, and reign alone,
> The Lord of every motion there!

Trade Unions

There is, however, an even closer parallel between conditions in Thyatira and those of our own days. The counterparts of the trade guilds which existed in Thyatira are to be found in our western civilisation but we call them trade unions. Trade unions were formed to advance the living standards of their members and succeeded in rectifying many injustices. After considerable experience, trade unions decided that they could only achieve their objectives through a political party and so (in Britain) the Labour party was formed. This party is largely controlled by them and a Labour party leader could not survive unless supported by the unions. They also largely finance the Labour party, not only through the political levy paid by union members (unless they contract out) but also from general union funds. Legislation has given unions the power to insist that employment in a particular factory or industry is restricted to their members; a worker can be deprived of his union card for various reasons and then finds it extremely difficult if not impossible to obtain alternative employment. A person refusing to join a union can be debarred from employment where a 'closed shop' exists. So it is as necessary today for workers to belong to the appropriate trade unions as it was for their predecessors in Thyatira to be members of the trade guilds.

What ought to be the attitude of believers to trade unions? Clearly (and this is not the place to discuss this in detail; readers are referred to the pamphlet *The Gospel and Strife* by Brother A. D. Norris and to *The Christadelphian*, May 1981, p.186), they cannot join actively in the work of a trade union or contribute to its political fund because this would be to take an active part in politics which we have always abjured. But what of 'sleeping' membership of a trade union when the subscription is paid but no part taken in its activities? Can we find guidance from the experience of our Thyatiran brethren and sisters? We, like them, must keep ourselves from idols and worship one God only. We must not follow Jezebel in acknowledging more than one God.

Political Involvement

The often violent and inconsiderate action taken to further trade union ambitions and their virtual control of a major political party, indicate that they worship the god of power. They try to force the government of the day to follow their policies. They are immersed in political activities. A believer joining a trade union even as a passive member by that act shares this worship. It may be very difficult for someone who became a member before trade union political ambitions and militancy developed to the current level to take advantage of recent legislation permitting him to with-

THE LETTER TO THYATIRA

draw from his union, and pay the amount of his union subscription to a charity approved by the union, but some may feel impelled to do so whatever the cost. Young believers about to commence work should carefully consider the Lord's letter to Thyatira and seek to avoid problems similar to those created there by the trade guilds by contracting out of union membership from the outset of their working lives: "In the absence of any central Christadelphian authority it is impossible to legislate for the attitude of individual members to the question of Trade Union membership; they exercise their freedom of conscience. Many of them interpret the Christadelphian attitude described above as a complete barrier to such membership and cannot in conscience join a Trade Union. We would strongly support any who feel obliged to take this standpoint" (*The Christadelphian*, 1981, p. 188).

The Lord's exhortation to Thyatira comes down to us over the centuries: Take a firm grip on what you have and keep my works until the end. We believe we are now very near the end of this age and we ought to pay closer attention to what we have heard, lest we drift away from it (Hebrews 2:1). We can be seduced from the Faith by the plausible ideas of men, as were some of the Thyatiran believers, and try to find a 'reasonable' compromise with those around us, as some of them did, even if it means the modern equivalent of fornication and eating things sacrificed to idols. Those who keep his works will reject any compromise that would endanger their belief or manner of life, while always remembering that this staunchness must be combined with tact and graciousness in dealing with those in error or the people among whom we live and work. Keeping our Lord's works to the end will not be achieved by an occasional victory over a major temptation but in the daily overcoming of our weaknesses and the exhibition of his character in our humdrum lives.

The god of this world can still blind the eyes of believers and we must therefore try to examine ourselves through the eyes of Jesus, to see ourselves as the Lord sees us. The letters to these ecclesias help us to do this.

> Search us, O God, and know each heart,
> With every idol bid us part.

7

THE LETTER TO SARDIS

SARDIS, a little more than 30 miles from Thyatira, was one of the great cities of primitive history. Situated on a small plateau on the northern slope of Mount Tmolus, it overlooked the great plain of the Hermus over 1500 feet below. Sardis was inaccessible except from the south; the rock walls on all other sides were smooth, nearly perpendicular and regarded as unscalable. The southern approach was difficult and with soldiers guarding it the city was virtually impregnable. It was therefore the natural capital of the great Kingdom of Lydia; the city was a meeting point of the ancient system of roads and its great wealth resulted from trade, especially with the East, and the careful cultivation of the fertile soil of the Hermus valley.

Sardis was the centre of trade in wool and woollen fabrics. The art of dyeing, for which Thyatira became noted, was invented in Sardis, which was also famous for a metal called electrum, probably an alloy similar to bronze. Trade with the East would inevitably decline when the new major route from Ephesus to the East, which did not go near Sardis, came into use (see Chapter 1).

One of the most famous and wealthy of the Lydian kings was Croesus, who was defeated in battle by Cyrus the Great. Croesus retired to his impregnable fortress at Sardis while he raised fresh armies to attack the Persians but a Median soldier found a way up the steep sides of the plateau and led the Persians into Sardis. A few men on guard could have repelled the Persians but they were not there and Cyrus came upon the city "like a thief in the night". The lesson was not learned. Some three centuries later, Antiochus the Great besieged Sardis and again the garrison, in careless self-confidence, guarded only the one established route into the citadel, believing that the steep sides would not be

THE LETTER TO SARDIS

climbed. But history repeated itself and in 218 B.C. a Cretan soldier led Antiochus' army up an 'unscalable' approach.

After the Persian conquest, Sardis became the seat of the governor of Asia Minor. Alexander the Great conquered the Persians in 334 B.C. and made Sardis into an autonomous self-governing city of the Greek type. Two centuries or so later, Sardis passed into Roman hands. In A.D. 17, the city, with twelve others, was devastated by a great earthquake but rebuilt with very generous aid from the Emperor Tiberius. Sardis joined with other cities ruined by the earthquake in erecting a monument to Tiberius in acknowledgement of his munificence. It competed with, but lost to Smyrna for the privilege of erecting a temple for the worship of Tiberius though the cult of Emperor worship must have been strong in Sardis. The city expanded on to the plain and remained important in Roman times but did not regain its former glory.

The patron deity of Sardis was Cybele, whose worship (as we have seen) was accompanied by gross immorality. The cult of Cybele was joined to that of the Emperor and there was a strong Jewish element in the city. Croesus is said to have advised Cyrus after the latter had captured Sardis to discourage the martial spirit of the Lydians by employing them only in those arts which ministered to luxury and sensuality. Cyrus reportedly took this advice and the Lydians became effeminate and lacking energy. Certainly the Sardians had a bad reputation in antiquity for luxury and loose living.

A Letter Without Commendation

With this background, we turn to the Lord's letter to the ecclesia in Sardis (Revelation 3:1-6). Notice first how the Lord introduced himself. He had *"the seven spirits of God"*; *"in him the whole fulness of deity dwells bodily"* (Colossians 2:9). This all-powerful and omniscient One had the seven stars, the seven ecclesias in his power and exactly assessed their spiritual state. His judgement could not be challenged nor his power to act as he saw ecclesial conditions required. *"I know your works."*

In the first four letters the Lord commenced with commendation for the things he could praise. There is no such introductory commendation in the letter to Sardis. No severer indictment could have been brought against an ecclesia than that against Sardis. The key phrase which will help us understand this is: *"I have not found your works perfect in the sight of my God."* The word translated "perfect" (*pleroō*) means "filled up" (cf. Matthew 23:32— *"Fill ye up then the measure of your fathers"*; John 12:3— *"The house was filled with the fragrance of the perfume"*; cf. John 15:11; 16:2,24 etc.). "Works" in the earlier letters included toil, patient endurance, love, faith, service. None of these works in Sardis was brought to completion; all were half-performed (cf. Luke 8:14). The Lord is not here referring to the absolute perfection a believer cannot achieve in this life but to a shortfall in what they could and should have done. Notice also the contrast between the Lord in whom *"all the fulness of God was pleased to dwell"* (Colossians 1:19) and their own partially filled state (fulness, *pleroma*, the noun corresponding to the verb *pleroō*).

"The name of being alive"

"You have the name of being alive and you are dead." Sardis was held in high reputation by the other ecclesias. Heresy and immorality were not charged against her; there were no Nicolaitans or Balaamites there, nor a Jezebel to corrupt its members. The outward forms of their religion were observed. In the eyes of the other meetings they were a model ecclesia, alive and their works fulfilled but *their* assessment was not the criterion by which the Lord evaluated them: *"I have not found your works*—the phrase means 'any of your works'—*perfect **in the sight of my God**."* What mattered at Sardis was how God regarded their works rather than the other ecclesias. The elders at Sardis and the bulk of the ecclesia had no idea that they were dead. They were not without works and had unwittingly misled themselves as well as other ecclesias. They held the form of religion but denied its power (2 Timothy 3:5).

Death is repeatedly used figuratively in Scripture to describe man's natural state (e.g. Matthew 8:22; John 5:25). At baptism, the believers at Sardis had been made alive, when they were dead in trespasses and sins (Ephesians 2:1,5; cf. Romans 6:11;

THE LETTER TO SARDIS

Colossians 1:13). Henceforth they were to live as men who had been brought from death to life (Romans 6:13). They had to walk in the spirit and not *"gratify the desires of the flesh. For the desires of the flesh are against the spirit, and the desires of the spirit are against the flesh; for these are opposed to each other . . . the works of the flesh are plain: immorality, impurity, licentiousness, idolatry, sorcery, enmity, strife, jealousy, anger, selfishness, dissension, party spirit, envy, drunkenness, carousing, and the like"* (Galatians 5:16,17,19-21). If they lived according to these, they would die (Romans 8:13). Believers had been created in Christ Jesus for good works (Ephesians 2:10), to produce in their lives the fruit of the spirit, *"love, joy, peace, patience, kindness, goodness, faithfulness, gentleness, self-control"* (Galatians 5:22-23) for *"by this my Father is glorified, that you bear much fruit, and so prove to be my disciples"* (John 15:8).

None of these works of the flesh is charged against Sardis and yet they were dead; although they had resisted the grosser sins in the society around them, they had succumbed without realising it to its insidious influence in another way. They had forgotten that *"she who is self-indulgent is dead even while she lives"*; that *"faith by itself, if it has no works, is dead"* (1 Timothy 5:6; James 2:17,26).

Muted Witness

We can best understand this if we remind ourselves of the character of the inhabitants of Sardis. They were careless and had grown slack and self-indulgent with luxurious living. The ecclesia, while resisting the grosser temptations, had allowed this spirit of the society in which they lived to influence them. They too were self-indulgent and had not put their necks to the work of their Lord. Why had this happened? There is no mention in the letter of persecution or hardship to be endured. Their metal had not been proved in the fire of affliction. This suggests that their witness to Jesus as Messiah, their testimony against Emperor or idol worship and to the manner of life required of the Christian were so muted as not to arouse the antagonism of Jew or Gentile. They had avoided persecution by their half-hearted witness to the Gospel.

As we have seen earlier, the authorities would readily accept a new religious cult if it could be fitted into the pantheon of existing religions. It looks as though the elders at Sardis had avoided hardship by toning down their witness to Christ, thus making their Christianity so emasculated that it presented no threat to the society in which they lived; in effect the two had reached a tacit understanding. On the one hand, the ecclesia maintained its muted witness and on the other, society let it alone, knowing that such witness was harmless. This attitude produced spiritual torpor in the ecclesia. Their service was half-hearted and the Christian virtues only partly cultivated. They had become complacent, maintaining an outward appearance but with no real life within.

The Modern Sardis

Let us pause and examine ourselves in the light of the Lord's comments on Sardis. It is possible for a modern ecclesia to be in a position similar to that at Sardis. We may be apparently irreproachable, properly organised, punctilious in attending the meetings and so on. These are essential to ecclesial life; they were in evidence at Sardis or that ecclesia could not have enjoyed the reputation it had, but the truth about Sardis was very different from its reputation. It may be so with us; like our brethren and sisters at Sardis, most of us do not have persecution to prove our metal. Again, like them, we live in a self-indulgent and self-pleasing society with a spirit expressed by the phrase, 'I couldn't care less'. Like them, we may resist the immorality around us but succumb gradually and unconsciously to this spirit.

We begin our career in the Truth with enthusiasm and zeal but the years pass, the response to our preaching is meagre, problems arise in ecclesial life and the Lord does not come. Imperceptibly our efforts may slacken and we tend to leave our work only partly done. Our toil, endurance and zeal, our love, faith and service alike diminish. Bible study becomes superficial, and preparation for an address is done a few hours before it is to be given. We do not base it on real Bible study because we have not left ourselves time for this. We become reluctant to undertake work for the ecclesia; such work takes many forms and there is something we can all do if we are prepared to give the necessary time. Our good

THE LETTER TO SARDIS

intentions are so often not "filled up" because we become more interested in the new car we are hoping to buy, or in the latest hi-fi or video equipment or other hobbies, than in our Lord's service, and this reduces the time we have for that service which inevitably becomes half-done.

Is this a picture of our ecclesia? We must not become nominal Christadelphians, just keeping in touch so that our name is not on the absence list. Natural Israel failed to give God the best of their flocks but offered blind, lame, or sick animals in sacrifice. Present such *"to your governor,"* said God; *"will he be pleased with you?"* (Malachi 1:8). Would our employer accept the quality of the work we offer to God or reject it as inadequate? The new Israel must not fail as did natural Israel; we must not allow our Lord's verdict on us to be that which he passed on Sardis. The Truth must not become a mere addendum to our other interests instead of life's main purpose and thus fail to bear fruit to maturity.

A Self-Indulgent Society

Another aspect of the self-indulgent society in which we live is the lack of respect, and this may affect our attitude to God. We may come into His presence almost as into that of an equal, presuming to approach God directly and not through Jesus, forgetting that we are by nature "of unclean lips" and that approach into His most holy presence is a precious privilege which we must never take for granted. If we fail to realise that the ground on which we stand before God in prayer and worship is most holy and do not in our worship give God the reverence due to Him, such worship will be imperfect, not "filled up" in His sight.

Lack of respect is shown by some around us in the extreme informality of the clothes worn and the fashions followed. A book was recently published to help young people at interviews for a job. The advice given was, "Go looking respectable and reasonably dressed (i.e. conventional)" (*The Daily Telegraph*, 15.2.82). Ought we to approach the God of Heaven dressed in a way a potential employer would find unacceptable? Some may be tempted to go to the other extreme and forget Paul's instructions to sisters to adorn themselves modestly and sensibly in seemly apparel (1 Timothy 2:9). Aaron's priestly garments were "to give him dignity and honour" (Exodus 28:2, N.I.V.). The analogy may not be exact but believers will not go far wrong if what they wear gives dignity with reverence in their approach to God.

There are other aspects of the society around us which can adversely affect our lives in Christ so insidiously that we do not realise what is happening. A healthy spiritual life demands constant self-examination through the eyes of Jesus. It is easy to be satisfied with ourselves but much more difficult to "fill up" our works in God's sight. We must learn the lesson of Sardis and not become Christadelphians in name only, rendering half-hearted service. Let a man examine himself and let anyone who thinks that he stands take heed lest he fall.

The condition of the ecclesia has been described. Now comes the searching exhortation: *"Awake, and strengthen what remains and is on the point of death."* "Awake": the Greek implies "become awake". The word so translated (*gregoreō*) can be rendered either "watch" (A.V. and R.V.) or "awake" (R.S.V.). In Gethsemane Jesus asked the three disciples to watch, to keep awake with him. Paul instructed the elders of Ephesus "to be alert" (R.S.V.), to "watch" (A.V. and R.V.). And to the Thessalonians, he said: *"Let us not sleep . . . but let us keep awake"* (R.S.V.). The meaning of the Lord's command to Sardis is well expressed in Weymouth's translation: *"Rouse yourself and keep awake, and strengthen what still remains though it is on the point of death"*. Peter was bidden to strengthen his brethren; Paul went through Galatia and Phrygia strengthening all the disciples (cf. 1 Thessalonians 3:2,13; 2 Thessalonians 2:17; 3:3).

These were encouraged not merely to hold fast in face of adversity but to develop to the full the qualities of the Christian life. The angel, the elders, were told to bestir themselves, to fan into flame the smouldering embers, to complete their half-done works. Note the Lord's love and care, even for Sardis. What remained was on the point of death and would die if not strengthened. The Lord wrote to the elders to give them a last opportunity of so doing.

THE LETTER TO SARDIS

The Command to Remember

"Remember then what (or how) you received and heard; keep that, and repent." "Remember": the command is the same as to Ephesus but whereas the Ephesians were instructed to remember from what they had fallen, repent and do the works they did at first, the elders at Sardis were told to remember *how*, after what manner they had received the Truth. There is a mixture of tenses in this verse. "Remember" implies that they should go on remembering, always keep in mind how they had received the Gospel.

"Received" refers to the deposit of doctrine and manner of life they had been given at baptism and which had not been contaminated by heresy. Sardis kept *what* had been committed to their care but had lost the zeal and heartiness with which they had received it (cf. 1 Thessalonians 1:5-10; Hebrews 10:32). The word "received" is used in the parable of the talents given to the master's servants for use on his behalf, a service from which they could not opt out or retire and remain faithful servants. The use of the same word to Sardis would remind them of their solemn duty to use to the full the talents their Master had committed to them (cf. Colossians 2:6-7).

"Hold fast, and repent"

"And heard" refers to the act of hearing when they received the Gospel. "Keep that" means "keep all the time what you received and heard". "Keep" is one of John's favourite words and he used it more frequently than any other New Testament writer. The Lord kept his Father's commandments, His word. The disciple keeps the Lord's words, his commandments (John 8:51,52,55; 14:15,21,23,24; 15:10; 17:6; 1 John 2:3,5; 3:22,24; 5:3; Revelation 1:3; 2:26; 3:8; 12:17; 22:7,9). "Keep" clearly means keep absolutely, without equivocation or relaxation.

"And repent" is a command for an urgent act of reformation, a return to their original condition when no labour for the Truth had been too much bother. *"If you will not awake"* or "If, however, you fail to rouse yourself and keep awake": 'If you do not heed my command I will come like a thief, stealthily,

THE LETTERS TO THE SEVEN CHURCHES OF ASIA

unexpectedly, and you will not know at what hour I will come upon you.'

These words would remind the ecclesia of the Lord's Mount Olivet prophecy, which clearly made a great impression on the disciples who heard it and on the early church to whom they transmitted it, for the unexpected thieflike return of the Lord is repeatedly referred to in the apostolic writings (1 Thessalonians 5:2,4; 2 Peter 3:10; Revelation 16:15). *"Watch, therefore*—keep awake—*for you do not know on what day your Lord is coming. But know this, that if the householder had known in what part of the night the thief was coming, he would have watched*—kept awake—*and would not have let his house be broken into." "And what I say to you I say to all: Watch*—keep awake—*lest he come suddenly and find you asleep"* (Matthew 24:42-43; Mark 13:37,36).

"I will come like a thief"

Similar language was used to warn the brethren and sisters at Sardis, although here it refers to an act of judgement on the ecclesia, as at Ephesus and Pergamum, rather than to the Lord's return. If they did not repent and keep awake, they would be taken by surprise when the Lord came to them in judgement. The Lord's words must also have reminded the ecclesia of the time when Cyrus came on Sardis like a thief in the night and caught the city unprepared, because no-one was on the look-out. A similar disaster threatened the ecclesia if the brethren and sisters did not rouse themselves and keep awake. The remedy for natural drowsiness is to get up and do something; similarly the remedy for spiritual drowsiness is to become active in the Lord's service. How often, directly or by implication, the Lord returned to the need for them to do this.

A few very understanding words follow: *"Yet you have still a few names in Sardis, people who have not soiled their garments."* The figure used is similar to that in the prologue to John's Gospel. The Lord came unto his own who received him not. This was true as a broad generalisation but there were exceptions to it, for to all who received him he gave the right to become children of God (John 1:11-12). So here. As a generalisation the ecclesia was dead, but a few members were still alive. The Lord assured them they had not been overlooked and were not included in his condemnation of the ecclesia. They had not soiled their garments. The word used (*molunein*) means to smear or smirch as with mud or filth and is used in the Septuagint of the staining of Joseph's coat with blood (cf. Isaiah 59:3).

How had the majority of the ecclesia soiled their garments in view of the absence of any charge of immorality against them? Because, in Jude's words, they had not hated even the garment spotted by the flesh (Jude 23). The flesh soiled their garments when they permitted the spirit of ease and self-indulgence in society around them to influence them and prevent their works in the Truth from being brought to completion. They had not lived up to the profession made at the time of baptism; they had not fulfilled the figure of baptism and *"crucified the flesh with its . . . desires"* (Galatians 5:24). The Lord here plainly indicates that believers' garments can be soiled by allowing the spirit of society adversely to influence them as well as by immorality. He thus reinforced his earlier criticism of the ecclesia.

The lesson for modern believers is obvious. We can only repeat what has already been said. We must not allow the society in which we live in any way adversely to affect our lives and service in the Truth. In our preaching, we ought not to over-emphasise prophetic forecasts and the like at the expense of the basic Gospel theme of repentance from dead works because we think the latter may be less acceptable to those around us. Our primary task is to hold forth the word of life both to those without and those who have accepted the Gospel.

"Thou hast a few names"

A further point is worthy of notice. The few who had not soiled their garments were not instructed to withdraw from the ecclesia. The Lord did not regard the state of affairs at Sardis as warranting separation. Rather, those who had not soiled their garments had the task of helping to revivify the ecclesia, infusing life into what was on the point of death. This would be difficult, laborious and often frustrating, but there was no alternative if the position at Sardis was to be restored. Here is an example for believers today if they ever face a similar situation.

One final thought. We believe that Jesus is about to return to the earth and his Mount Olivet prophecy rings down the centuries, sounding a warning to us. Watch, keep awake, for we do not know the day of our Lord's coming, lest coming suddenly, unexpectedly, he find us drowsing. The parable of the ten virgins indicates that some will not be prepared to meet him and the succeeding parable shows that disciples prepare for his return by the diligent use of the talents entrusted to them. If we fail to do this we shall not be ready to meet him, however diligently we may have studied prophecies of the end and scanned the political heavens for the sign of his coming. The Lord used the language of his Mount Olivet prophecy to warn the believers at Sardis of impending judgement if they did not repent. His words apply equally to those living at the time of his return.

Rouse yourselves, keep awake and strengthen what remains. If we fail to do so, he will come upon us as a thief. *"Blessed are those servants whom the Master finds awake when he comes; truly I say to you, he will gird himself and have them sit at table, and he will come and serve them"* (Luke 12:37; cf. Revelation 16:15). God grant that in the day of his coming, we may be found awake, active in his service and permitted to share his table.

8

THE LETTER TO PHILADELPHIA

PHILADELPHIA was not an ancient city with a long history like Sardis; it was founded in the second century B.C. by King Attalus Philadelphus and called Philadelphia in his honour. The city was situated in the valley of the river Cogamis on the slopes of Mount Timolus about 28 miles from Sardis. The Cogamis was an important tributary of the river Hermus which it joined just above Sardis. Trade from the harbour at Smyrna went by road through Sardis to Philadelphia and the East. This trade route divided at Philadelphia, one branch going north-east through Phrygia and the other south-east to the cities of the Lycus valley. This road system was second only in importance to the great trade route from Ephesus to the East.

Philadelphia was situated in an old volcanic district, surrounded by mountains and subject to earthquakes. It was founded for the spread of the Greek language and culture in Lydia and Phrygia for which it was well suited by its location but it made little impression on the old deep-rooted nature worship.

Imperial City

The city soon passed under Roman rule and was a place of importance in the imperial organisation of the province of Asia, although less so than the other six cities. When John wrote, the imperial post-road from Rome to the East passed through the city which, like Sardis, received generous help from Tiberius after the great earthquake of A.D. 17 which devastated it. Shocks were experienced for a long while after the earthquake, causing many of the inhabitants to leave the city and live outside it in tents, huts and booths. The city changed its name in honour of Tiberius (to Neocaesarea) for the help he gave and again later in honour of Vespasian (to Flavia) but ultimately reverted to its original name.

THE LETTERS TO THE SEVEN CHURCHES OF ASIA

The soil, as is often the case in such areas, was very fertile and especially suited to grape-growing. Philadelphia thus became famous for its wines and, despite the risks, people continued to live there because of the fertile soil, just as they do in certain volcanic areas of Italy today. One of its deities was naturally Dionysus—Bacchus—the god of wine. There were hot springs in the area in which the infirm came to bathe, much as people used to do in the medicinal waters of Bath.

With this preamble, we turn to the Lord's letter to the ecclesia in Philadelphia.

"Holy and true"

There are obvious similarities between the position of the ecclesias in Philadelphia and Smyrna. They are the only ecclesias to receive unqualified praise from their Lord. They were free from heresy and moral failings despite the worship of Dionysus at Philadelphia which could have corrupted the brethren and sisters. Smyrna was poor and Philadelphia had but little power. Both faced active opposition from Jews who, unlike these ecclesias, were rich and powerful. Smyrna was about to suffer tribulation but Philadelphia had already been tested. He who died and came to life identified himself with those in Smyrna who would suffer death but receive the crown of life. Unlike the preceding letter, there is no direct allusion in this letter to the Lord's descriptions and titles in Revelation 1, but how appropriate was the Lord's introduction to it. He was *"the holy one, the true one"*. "The Holy One" is a title of God (Isaiah 40:25; Habakkuk 3:3) and elsewhere in Revelation is used of God (4:8; 6:10; 15:4; 16:5). The application of this title to Jesus would remind the ecclesia that, although they had but little power, they served the one who bore God's titles, to whom God had given all power in heaven and earth.

"The true one": The word translated "true" does not mean true as opposed to false but that which is perfect contrasted with the imperfect or incomplete. Used here, it means that whatever title is given to Jesus—the true light, the true bread from heaven, the true vine—is realised to the full in him. He is all he claims to

THE LETTER TO PHILADELPHIA

be, absolutely genuine. And he finds a similar quality in the ecclesia. They had been true to their Lord. They had kept his word and had not denied his name. They were genuine in the profession of their faith, their heart was true (Hebrews 10:22). How encouraged this ecclesia of little power would be to know that the holy one, the true one, who knew their works, had given them unqualified approval.

"Who has the key of David, who opens and no one shall shut, who shuts and no one opens": These words are almost a direct citation from Isaiah 22. The prophet there speaks of the rejection of Shebna, who was over Hezekiah's household and his replacement by Eliakim. *"In that day I will call my servant Eliakim the son of Hilkiah, and I will clothe him with your robe, and bind your girdle on him, and will commit your authority to his hand; and he shall be a father to the inhabitants of Jerusalem and to the house of Judah. And I will place on his shoulder the key of the house of David; he shall open, and none shall shut; and he shall shut and none shall open"* (vv. 20-22).

"Who shuts and no one opens"

The Lord's application of these words to himself indicates that he alone had absolute power over the house of David, that he was the one to whom God would give the throne of David and who would reign over the house of Jacob for ever. Consider the background in Philadelphia against which the Lord's words were spoken. We do not know how the Truth reached Philadelphia but if the usual practice was followed, the Gospel would first be preached to the Jews in the city (e.g. Acts 13:46). Hence some, perhaps many members of the ecclesia, would be Jews from the synagogue who had accepted Jesus as the Messiah. This would enrage the other Jews, who closed the doors of the synagogue to the Jewish converts, ostracised, despised and persecuted them. Associations, perhaps of many years, would be broken and friends lost. The converts would suffer much heartache.

We saw in the Introduction that Christianity was initially regarded by Rome as an offshoot of Judaism and therefore exempt from emperor worship. This immunity ceased before John wrote and the excommunication of Jewish believers from the

THE LETTERS TO THE SEVEN CHURCHES OF ASIA

synagogue therefore exposed them to Roman persecution. The Jews regarded the Kingdom as for them only and thought that by excommunicating Jewish believers in Christ they had closed the door of the Kingdom of God to them, but the Lord reminded them that the Jews did not have the power to do this. He, and he alone, had the authority to admit to or exclude from the Kingdom. When he acts, none can thwart him.

In one of the loveliest psalms, God is thus described: *"He healeth the broken in heart, and bindeth up their wounds. He telleth the number of the stars; he giveth them all their names. Great is our Lord and mighty in power. His understanding is infinite"* (Psalm 147:2-5, R.V.). Jesus, the perfect exemplar of God, showed both these facets of the divine nature. The vision in Revelation 1 and the opening words of this letter describe the One who is great and mighty in power but this is followed by his binding up the wounds of the brethren and sisters in Philadelphia. He knew what they had endured for his sake and understood their feelings and comforted them by the reminder that these unpleasantnesses were transient: he possessed the key of the house of David and would in due time open the door of the kingdom to them. His understanding of them and their problems was infinite—beyond measure. The Lord in glory had the same compassion and understanding as in the days of his flesh.

Suffering for the Name

Let us pause for a moment to think of modern believers. A century ago those who accepted the Truth were often ostracised, suffered loss in business and sometimes faced active persecution. Today people may regard us as peculiar because we go each Sunday to our meeting and try to live Christian lives; but only rarely are we ostracised or caused to suffer because of our allegiance to Christ. Nonetheless, there are times when we suffer heartache from other causes. Sooner or later, believers experience unpleasantness in their lives, even their lives in the Truth. When such come to us, we must remember that, come what may, whatever our experiences, the Lord we serve is still one whose understanding of us is infinite.

THE LETTER TO PHILADELPHIA

The Lord continues: *"I know your works. Behold, I have set before you an open door"*: The door of the synagogue had been closed against them but the Lord had opened a door no human power could close. Jesus may be telling them again that entrance into the Kingdom is his alone to give by reminding them of his saying: *"I am the door; by me if any man enter in, he shall be saved"* (John 10:9). However, the figure of an opened door is often used in the New Testament to denote a door opened for preaching the Gospel (Acts 14:27; 1 Corinthians 16:9; 2 Corinthians 2:12; Colossians 4:3) and the opened door here probably refers primarily to an opportunity the Lord had set before them for such work. We mentioned earlier that Philadelphia was founded for the spread of Greek language and culture although it had not been very successful in this. Its situation at the crossroads of the trade routes, with a constant influx of travellers, made it a good centre for evangelism.

"I know that you have but little power." At Philadelphia, as at Corinth earlier, not many powerful persons were called because God chose what is weak in the world to shame the strong (1 Corinthians 1:26-27). The Lord's power is made perfect in weakness (2 Corinthians 12:9) and the Philadelphian believers had won strength out of weakness (Hebrews 11:34). Put to the test—the tense of the Greek verb (aorist) indicates occasion(s) in the past when this had happened—they had kept his word, remained faithful to his teaching and not denied his name. At Smyrna the test had still to come but here it had been surmounted. The Lord knew that they had but little power but did not blame them for this because it was due to causes outside their control. Like Mary, they had done what they could (Mark 14:8). If we may borrow the language of the parable, Philadelphia was a one talent ecclesia but, unlike the servant in the parable, they had used it to the full and were commended for this.

Again, how perfectly Jesus understood them! As a result of their fidelity, the meeting, probably few in number and certainly of little power, was given an opened door for their preaching by the One mighty in power and no human adversary could close it. How appropriate that, where their adversaries were primarily

THE LETTERS TO THE SEVEN CHURCHES OF ASIA

Jewish, the ecclesia was told that the door had been opened by the One who had the Key of David! So they were encouraged to continue to use their one talent to the full and seize the opportunity the Lord had provided for effective work (1 Corinthians 16:9) as they had earlier opportunities. What a contrast with the half-hearted ecclesia at Sardis and the spiritual poverty at Laodicea!

Opportunities Seized

And what an example for modern believers. The Lord still opens doors, he is active today as he was 1900 years ago. Are we using those doors for proclaiming the Gospel? 1900 years ago an opportunity came to an ecclesia which had little power but it was seized. There are many small ecclesias throughout the world today struggling year after year to continue their work for the Lord. Sometimes they barely maintain their numbers after decades of preaching. Jesus knows they have but little power: his understanding of them is still infinite, and he does not expect a one talent meeting to produce results possible for a five talent meeting but he does require that, as at Philadelphia, they will do all they can by making full use of their one talent.

The temptation to which a believer or an ecclesia is subject if they have but one talent, is not to use it, thinking that it cannot make any real difference whether the talent is used or buried. The Philadelphian ecclesia had not succumbed to this temptation and left an example for meetings of each succeeding generation who find themselves in a similar position. The message of this letter to such ecclesias is that they need not thereby be discouraged. Their Lord understands their lack of power and will commend them in the day of judgement if they had made full use of what they had. There is also a message for larger ecclesias today. They too must make full use of the doors the Lord opens for his work. It is easy in a large ecclesia to leave others to do the work. There is always someone who will! This attitude of leaving it to others and not doing all that we can is not one which will meet with the Lord's approval when he comes to reckon with his servants.

"You have kept my word." The value and authority of the word of Christ have been greatly diminished in the last century or more

by those around us. We must take great care not to be affected by this attitude.

"You have not denied my name." It is possible for a modern believer to be a member of an ecclesia and yet to deny the name of Jesus because his manner of life is inconsistent with his profession of Christ. So far as is humanly possible, we must allow him to bring thought, word and action increasingly into obedience to him.

"Behold, I will make those of the synagogue of Satan who say that they are Jews and are not, but lie—behold, I will make them come and bow down before your feet, and learn that I have loved you". The Lord's promise was not that all of the synagogue of Satan would come and bow down to them but, as the Greek idiom requires, some of the synagogue would do so (*Speaker's Commentary*, quoting Winer). There is a delightful irony in the words the Lord used. They are reminiscent of several passages in Isaiah (45:14; 49:23; 60:14) where the prophet foretold Gentile submission to the Jews, which Jews were then eagerly anticipating but which is still future. The Lord here used the prophet's words not to describe the obeisance of Gentiles to Jews but that of some of the synagogue of Satan to the believers. They would acknowledge that the Jewish Christians had been right after all!

"And learn that I have loved you." The pronoun "I" is emphatic in the Greek. Again these words are quoted from the prophets (Isaiah 43:4; Malachi 1:2) where they are applied to Israel. How those Jewish Christians would appreciate these promises and especially the language in which the Lord expressed them! It may be that their complete fulfilment awaits the re-establishment of the throne of David but words used by Ignatius some 20 years later suggest that there could have been an influx of Jews into the ecclesia. This is one of many questions to which we shall not know the answer until the Lord returns.

"Because you have kept my word of patient endurance, I will keep you from the hour of trial which is coming on the whole world, to try those who dwell upon the earth." "My word of patient endurance" is literally, "the word of the endurance of me". John had reminded his readers that he shared with them the patient endurance (Revelation

1:9). The Lord was here referring primarily to his patient endurance as an example to believers. They had to look to the Lord who endured the cross and the hostility of sinners against himself (Hebrews 12:1-3). Jesus left believers an example that they should follow his steps (1 Peter 2:21-23). Like their Lord, they had need of endurance so that they might do the will of God (Hebrews 10:36). And so Paul prayed that the Lord would direct the hearts of believers *"to the steadfastness of Christ"*, literally, "the endurance of Christ". (The Greek word is the same as that used in Revelation 3:10.) Suffering produces endurance and endurance produces character (Romans 5:3-4). The Philadelphian believers had verified this in their own lives; the testing of their faith produced steadfastness and steadfastness had had its full effect, making them perfect and complete, lacking in nothing (James 1:3-4).

Out of Trials

Because they, on their part, had kept his word of patient endurance, the Lord on his part would keep them from the hour of trial which was coming on the whole world to try those who dwelt on the earth. The same Greek word translated "from" (*ek*, out of) is used in the Lord's prayer recorded in John 17. Jesus spoke of the men whom God had given him out of (*ek*) the world (v. 6). These men were physically still in the world (v. 11), and the Lord did not pray that his Father would literally take them out of the world in which they lived, but keep them from, out of, the evil in the world (v. 15). (The conjunction of the words translated "keep from" occurs only here and in Revelation 3:10.) The writer to the Hebrews says that *"Jesus offered up prayers and supplications, with loud cries and tears to him who was able to save him from* (*ek*, out of) *death, and he was heard for his godly fear"* (5:7). Jesus was not saved from dying but saved out of death. These Scripture usages suggest that the Lord did not promise to keep the Philadelphian believers untouched by the hour of trial but to bring them safely through, out of, the test. The all-powerful One would do this for those who had but little power because they had kept his word of patient endurance.

THE LETTER TO PHILADELPHIA

"I am coming soon". To understand the Lord's words regarding the hour of trial and his speedy return we must remember that he spoke from God's viewpoint, with whom one day is as a thousand years, and a thousand years as one day (2 Peter 3:8). Human time scales must not be applied to God's promises. The Lord's return was near in God's sight even if believers had to wait centuries for it. The Lord's words regarding the hour of trial which was about to come upon the Roman world are similar to those he used of the hour of trial immediately preceding his return. We shall have need of endurance, then, if we are to do the will of God and receive what is promised.

The Philadelphian believers could not be told that 1900 years or more would elapse before the final trial came or their morale, their power to endure, would have been destroyed. They would link the hour of trial with Trajan's persecution in the early years of the second century and hope this was the precursor of their Lord's return. They would thus be encouraged to hold fast.

The Believers' Crown

Today, human affairs appear to be heading for a catastrophe man cannot avert. The signs all seem to indicate our Lord's near return but we do not know its exact date. This lack of precise information should also keep modern believers on the alert but we must be prepared if the Lord does not come in our lifetime. He will come at the time God has fixed (Acts 17:31, R.S.V.) and, as we saw under Smyrna, his return will be heralded by an unprecedented time of trouble. When that comes, we must emulate the example of Philadelphia and keep the word of his patient endurance, showing in our lives in those very difficult days the endurance our Lord showed in his life on earth. If we on our part are patient until his coming, he on his part will keep us from, and bring us safely through the hour of trial. We too have need of endurance so that we may do the will of God and receive what is promised. *"For yet a little while and the coming one shall come and shall not tarry"* (Hebrews 10:36-37).

"That no one may seize your crown." The Lord is here alluding to Isaiah 22 from which he has already taken the symbol of the key of

THE LETTERS TO THE SEVEN CHURCHES OF ASIA

David. Shebna was told that God would take away his robe and his glorious crown and give them to Eliakim (v. 17, v. 21, LXX). God would not remove the crown from the Philadelphians but they could allow men to do so if they failed to hold fast what they had. The word translated "crown" in the verses in Isaiah 22 and Revelation 3 is *stephanos*, which means that which surrounds or encompasses and is usually used of a crown, wreath or garland, especially the victor's wreath at the public games (Liddell & Scott). It is used in this sense by Paul in 1 Corinthians 9:25. The Greek word for the crown of a king or emperor is *diadema*, translated in the R.V. and R.S.V. as "diadem" (Revelation 12:3; 13:1; 19:12) but the occurrences of *stephanos* in the LXX make it doubtful whether the distinction between that and *diadema* was strictly observed. *Stephanos* in the New Testament is also used as an emblem of the reward to come (James 1:12; 1 Peter 5:4) and of the successful work of Paul which he would wear like a crown at the Lord's coming (Philippians 4:1; 1 Thessalonians 2:19). The Lord here used the word to mean the reward, the prize which was in the grasp of the Philadelphians and which they would receive if they held fast what they had. The Lord would do his part and bring them through the hour of trial. They must do their part, continue in faithfulness and patient endurance, and the crown would be theirs for ever when the Lord came. None will then be able to seize it.

The Lord's words echo down the centuries to believers today. He is coming soon. We alone can loose our grip on the crown. How foolish modern believers would be to do this with the Lord at the door. Let us hold fast what we have that when the Lord comes, this crown will be ours for ever.

THE LETTER TO PHILADELPHIA

OCCURRENCES OF "CROWN" AND "TO CROWN" IN THE GREEK SCRIPTURES

In New Testament: **In Septuagint:**

Stephanos

Matthew 27:29; Mark 15:17; John 19:2,5; Philippians 4:1; 1 Thessalonians 2:19; 2 Timothy 4:8; James 1:12; 1 Peter 5:4; Revelation 2:10; 3:11; 4:4,10; 6:2; 9:7; 12:1; 14:14: all translated "crown" in R.S.V. Also in 1 Corinthians 9:25 where it is translated "wreath".

2 Samuel 12:30; 1 Chronicles 20:2; Esther 8:15; Job 19:9; 31:36; Psalm 20(21):3; 64(65):11; Proverbs 1:9; 4:9 (twice); 12:4; 14:24; 16:31; 17:6; Song of Solomon 3:11; Isa. 22:17,21; 28:1,3,5; 62:3; Jeremiah 13:18; Lamentations 2:15; 5:16; Ezekiel 16:12; 21:26; 23:42; 28:12; Zechariah 6:11,14.

Stephanoō (confer honour)

2 Timothy 2:5; Hebrews 2:7,9: all translated "crowned".

Psalm 5:12; 8:5; 102(103):4; Song of Solomon 3:11.

Diadema

Revelation 12:3; 13:1; 19:12: all translated "diadem" in R.S.V.

Esther 1:11; 2:17; 6:8 (Codex Sinaiticus only); 8:15; Isaiah 62:3.

(Chapters and verses in brackets refer to the slightly different numbering of the A.V.)

9

THE LETTER TO LAODICEA

LAODICEA was founded, or refounded, by Antiochus II in the third century B.C. and named after his wife. It was situated on a small plateau about 2 miles south of the river Lycus and often known as Laodicea on the Lycus to distinguish it from other cities of the same name. It was only six miles from Hierapolis and eleven from Colossae (cf. Colossians 4:13,16) and about 100 miles from Ephesus.

It occupied a strategic position where the narrow Lycus gorge opened into the broad plain of the Maeander river and a number of important roads met there. The great Eastern trade route from Miletus and Ephesus passed through it. The road from Pergamum in the north west through Thyatira and that from Smyrna joined at Sardis and continued to Laodicea. The roads to Attaleia and Perga in Pamphylia in the south east (Acts 14:25) and to Dorylaion in northern Phrygia ran from Laodicea. The city's sole weakness was the lack of a local water supply. Water had to be brought by aqueduct from hot springs several miles away and, if this was cut by an enemy, it made the city defenceless.

Banking, Wool and Medicine

Defence ceased to be important after 133 B.C. when Laodicea became part of the Roman empire. With peace guaranteed by Rome the city's importance and prosperity increased rapidly and it became a centre of banking and financial transactions and the most important centre of Roman jurisdiction in the province of Asia. Proconsular Courts were held there for the administration of justice. The remains of the aqueducts, a stadium and theatres testify to the magnificence of the city. It was devastated by the great earthquake of A.D. 17 already mentioned and, like other affected cities, received a generous grant from Tiberius to assist

THE LETTER TO LAODICEA

in rebuilding. Laodicea was again destroyed by an earthquake in A.D. 60 but this time refused the proffered Roman help. The citizens had resources of their own sufficient to rebuild the city without Roman assistance. They were rich and in need of nothing.

Laodicea derived its wealth from two other main sources besides banking. The area around the city was fertile and noted for sheep with a beautiful glossy black wool. An extensive and lucrative trade was carried on in garments and carpets woven from this wool. A large and famous school of medicine was associated with the temple of the local god (identified by the Greeks with Zeus). The temple was 13 miles west of Laodicea but the school of medicine was probably situated in the city itself and noted for its cures. It was the one famous medical centre in Phrygia. In particular, the physicians of Laodicea were skilful oculists and a preparation for weak eyes known as Phrygian powder was widely exported, usually in the form of cakes called *kollourion*.

Following the usual custom of the Seleucid kings, Antiochus II settled Jews in Laodicea, where they prospered. The amount of the temple tax remitted by them to Jerusalem in 62 B.C. indicates that there were then about 7,500 adult Jewish males in the locality, besides women and children. Julius Caesar permitted the Jews in Laodicea to observe their sabbaths and other sacred rites (Josephus, *Antiquities of the Jews*, Book 14, ch. 10, para. 20). As Laodicea increasingly prospered and became an important centre for financial transactions, the number of Jews there would grow and at the end of the first century A.D. there must have been a very substantial number in the city who exercised great influence.

How the Gospel Came to Laodicea

It is not known who brought the Gospel to Laodicea and the neighbouring cities. The evangelist was not Paul himself (Colossians 2:1) but his phraseology (Colossians 1:7-8 and 4:12) suggests that it might well have been Epaphras. There was a close relationship between the ecclesias at Colossae, Hierapolis and Laodicea (Colossians 4:13,16). The letter to Laodicea is very probably the letter known today as the epistle to the Ephesians. This may well have been a circular letter sent by Paul to several ecclesias in the area and the surviving copy is that which went to Ephesus; hence its title.*

We now turn to the Letter itself.

"The Amen." This is the only occasion when this word is used as a title of our Lord. It may be derived from Isaiah 65:16 where God is called the "God of Amen" (R.V. footnote). The R.V. and R.S.V. translate "God of Truth". The word is probably better referred to our Lord's repeated use of the word, especially in John's Gospel. The words translated "verily, verily" (A.V., R.V.) or "truly, truly" (R.S.V.) are in the Greek *amen, amen* and are used by our Lord when he is affirming a very important truth. *Amen* used by him here as a personal title guarantees the absolute truth of his testimony to Laodicea. This is reinforced by the words which follow.

"The faithful and true witness" (cf. Revelation 2:13). The word "witness" is repeatedly used by and of the Lord in John's Gospel. John in his introduction to the seven letters had already called Jesus "the faithful witness" (Revelation 1:5) but here the word "true" (*alethinos*) has been added. We need not repeat what was written under Philadelphia except to repeat that the word means that the Lord is all he claims to be, absolutely genuine. The combination of "faithful" and "true" emphasises the Lord's complete trustworthiness as a witness when he describes what he saw in the ecclesia.

---

* The words "at Ephesus" (Ephesians 1:1) are of doubtful authenticity and are omitted in the R.S.V. and other modern translations. Readers who wish to study the evidence for regarding "Ephesians" as the letter Paul sent to Laodicea can consult these books:

T. J. Barling, *The Letter to the Colossians*, pp. 44-45.
J. Rutherford, "The Epistle to the Laodiceans", *International Standard Bible Encyclopaedia*, 1930 edition, vol. 3, pp. 1836-1839.
J. Rutherford, *Paul's Epistles to Colossae and Laodicea*.
F. Foulkes, *The Epistle of Paul to the Ephesians* (Tyndale New Testament Commentaries), pp. 17ff.
J. O. F. Murray, *The Epistle to the Ephesians* (Cambridge Greek Testament for Schools and Colleges), pp. lxxvi-lxxviii.
(See also note on p. 31).

THE LETTER TO LAODICEA

"The beginning of God's creation." The words are reminiscent of Proverbs 8:22 (LXX) where it is written of Wisdom: *"The Lord made me the beginning of his ways for his works."* The Greek word *archē* is translated in the New Testament by a variety of words but mostly as "beginning". Grimm-Thayer give the first meaning as "beginning, origin" (Genesis 1:1, LXX; John 1:1; Matthew 19:4 etc.) and the second as "the person or thing that commences, the first person or thing in a series, the leader" (Colossians 1:18; Revelation 21:6; 22:13; cf. Deuteronomy 21:17, LXX; Job 40:14, LXX; Genesis 49:3, LXX). The Laodiceans had received the letter to the Colossians and therefore were familiar with Paul's phrase *"he (Jesus) is the beginning"*. The reference is to the beginning of God's creation because he is the firstborn of the dead. This is the new creation, the enduring and indestructible order brought into being by God who raised Christ to eternal life. Already, here and now, if a man be in Christ, *"he is a new creation; the old has passed away, behold the new has come"* (2 Corinthians 5:17).

"Christ is the *first* fruits of those who have fallen asleep (cf. 1 Corinthians 15:20), that in this matter, as in all others, he may be pre-eminent" (T. J. Barling, *The Letter to the Colossians*, p. 90).

"I know your works." The head of the new creation now makes a searching and severe but just examination of those who ought to have been, in truth as well as in name, part of the new creation. Notice first that no charge of heresy is brought against them. As at Sardis, there appear to have been no Nicolaitans, Balaamites or a Jezebel among them. But notice also that Laodicea, like Sardis, was free from active persecution. Despite the large Jewish community in the city there is no mention of a synagogue of Satan. This suggests that the ecclesia's witness to the Lord as the promised Messiah was, as at Sardis, sufficiently muted so as not to arouse the antagonism of the Jews.

"You are neither cold nor hot." The word translated "cold" (*psychros*) occurs outside this letter only in Matthew 10:42—*"And whoever gives to one of these little ones even a cup of cold water* (literally, 'of cold') *because he is a disciple, truly I say to you, he shall not lose his reward."* To us a cup of cold water is a trivial gift but circum-

stances were quite different in the very dry sub-tropical climate of Palestine. For the full enjoyment of water there, and indeed for health, it was doubly important to drink it cold. Water sellers carried cold spring water in vessels made of porous clay; the evaporation of the small amount of water which seeped through the container kept its contents cool. A cup of such cold water would be both welcome and necessary on a scorching hot day. (See Neil, *Everyday Life in the Holy Land*, pp. 169-171.) The Laodicean ecclesia was not providing refreshment for the spiritually weary (cf. 1 Corinthians 16:18; Philemon 7,20; 2 Timothy 1:16).

The word translated hot (*zestos*) occurs only in this letter and means boiling hot, bubbling up. A cognate word occurs in Acts 18:25 where Apollos is described as "fervent in spirit" (lit. "burning in spirit") and in Romans 12:11 where Paul exhorts the believers to *"be aglow with the spirit"*, "in spirit burning" (Marshall). The Lord's meaning in his letter to Laodicea is clear: they were not boiling, bubbling up with enthusiasm, burning in spirit for him.

"Would that you were cold or hot! So, because you are lukewarm, and neither cold nor hot, I will spew you out of my mouth." "Lukewarm" (*chliaros*) occurs only here in the New Testament. It is a rare Greek word and this is the only place in Greek literature where it is applied absolutely to persons.*

The Laodiceans were used to using lukewarm water because the city's water supply, brought from hot springs some miles away by aqueduct, arrived in a lukewarm condition. Such water was insipid and unrefreshing but they had to accept it. Hence they might have wondered how serious was the charge of lukewarmness had the Lord not told them the effect their lukewarmness had on him: *"I will spew you out of my mouth."* This is the only occurrence of the Greek word translated "spew" in the New Testament, but the ecclesia could not possibly miss the force

---

*All three words are applied in their literal sense more commonly to water than to anything else. This, and other information about the Greek words were obtained from an article by Rudwick and Green, *Expository Times*, 69 (1957-8) 176, although the writer does not accept their conclusions.

THE LETTER TO LAODICEA

of the Lord's words. Physicians in the famous school of medicine in the city used lukewarm water as an emetic. The ecclesia induced in Jesus a feeling of spiritual nausea just as lukewarm water produced physical nausea in patients who imbibed it and, therefore, "I will spew you out of my mouth", or "I have it in mind to vomit you out of my mouth."

The land of Canaan was said to have vomited out the original inhabitants and the incoming Israelites were warned to take care lest it vomit them out also (Leviticus 18:25,28; 20:22). The word "lukewarm" was chosen to indicate the effect the spiritual condition of the ecclesia had on Jesus rather than its spiritual temperature. The brethren and sisters were presented with the terrible reality of belonging to an ecclesia nauseous to its Lord and heading for complete rejection by him (cf. Revelation 2:5). The portrait Jesus painted was completely different from the picture they had of themselves but they could not challenge its authenticity. They could now see themselves as their Lord saw them. The Lord then tells the ecclesia why it produced this feeling in him.

"For (because), you say, I am rich, I have prospered, and I need nothing." Notice again how the attitude of the society in which an ecclesia lives can affect it. As we saw earlier, the city refused Roman aid in rebuilding after the great earthquake of A.D. 17. It was rich and in need of nothing. So the ecclesia thought itself spiritually rich and in need of nothing. It was proud and self-satisfied, blind to its true condition. The present tense "you say" means habitually say.

"I am rich, I have prospered" (R.V. "have gotten riches"). The inference is that they had acquired spiritual riches by their own efforts just as the city had become wealthy by its exertion. There is here an unmistakable allusion to Israel. *"Ephraim has said, Ah, but I am rich, I have gained wealth for myself"* (Hosea 12:8; cf. Zechariah 11:5; Deuteronomy 8:11 ff). Old and New Testament alike make it plain that such an attitude on the part of His people is abhorrent to God. Man can only be *"justified by his grace,* **as a gift**, *through the redemption which is in Christ Jesus"* (Romans 3:24). None has done or can do anything to merit in the slightest degree this divine grace.

"By grace you have been saved"

Notice how this is emphasised in Paul's letter to the Laodiceans. *"In him (Jesus) we have redemption through his blood, the forgiveness of our trespasses, according to the riches of his grace which he lavished upon us ... We all once lived in the passions of our flesh, following the desires of body and mind, and so we were by nature children of wrath, like the rest of mankind. But God, who is rich in mercy, out of the great love with which he loved us, even when we were dead through our trespasses, made us alive together with Christ (by grace you have been saved)".* He repeats this to emphasise its importance: *"For by grace you have been saved through faith; this is not your own doing, it is the gift of God—not because of works, lest any man should boast"* (Ephesians 1:7-8; 2:3-9; cf. Colossians 1:14).

Believers redeemed by God's grace are God's *"workmanship, created in Christ Jesus for good works"* (Ephesians 2:10). They are to *"work out your own salvation with fear and trembling, for God is at work in you, both to will and to work for his good pleasure"* (Philippians 2:12-13). The good works are of God. Both the will to do these works and the power to achieve them are alike attributed to God working in believers. Thus, although Paul worked harder than any of the other apostles, he acknowledged that *"it was not I, but the grace of God which is with me"* (1 Corinthians 15:10). His labours required much effort but he regarded them as the result of God working in him. Paul was an instrument of the grace of God and the praise for his works was therefore to be given to God and not to the apostle. He toiled, *"striving with all the energy which he mightily inspires in me"* (Colossians 1:29).

Believers, like Paul, are not left alone or they could not show the fruits of the spirit in their lives; they can draw on the limitless Divine power. Paul had reminded the Laodiceans of *"the immeasurable greatness of his (God's) power in us who believe, according to the working of his great might which he accomplished in Christ when he raised him from the dead and made him sit at his right hand"* (Ephesians 1:19-20). Jesus had been laid in the tomb of Joseph of Arimathea bruised, wounded, dead, but rose a glorified body made after the power of an endless life.

How great was the power which called Jesus from the grave and

THE LETTER TO LAODICEA

gave him the fulness of the Godhed bodily! This same mighty power had been at work in the Laodiceans and would continue to operate in their lives if they allowed it to do so. *"Now to him who by the power at work within us is able to do far more abundantly than all we ask or think"* (Ephesians 3:20). He who *"began a good work in you will perfect it until the day of Jesus Christ"* (Philippians 1:6, R.V.).

Children of the Light

Believers had their part to do: *"Let the word of Christ dwell in you richly"* (Colossians 3:16). The power of Christ could only operate to produce the fruit of the spirit in their lives if they allowed his word to dwell in them richly. Paul had told the Colossians that Christ was the image of the invisible God (1:15). In him, God's moral character was perfectly displayed. God spoke by a Son who reflects His glory and bears the very stamp of His nature (Hebrews 1:3). God had shined in the hearts of believers *"to give the light of the knowledge of the glory of God in the face of Christ"* (2 Corinthians 4:6). This was done so that believers, beholding this glory with unveiled face, could be changed into its likeness (2 Corinthians 3:18). Believers cannot make this light but, exposed to it, are increasingly transformed by it. Believers have this treasure in frail earthen vessels to show that the transforming power belongs to God and not to them, but the light that is at work in them will achieve its purpose unless they thwart it. The believers' task is to have a clear and bright vision of the glory of God in Christ through His word. They will not be transformed by this light if they take only an occasional view of it or if they put anything between them and the light to dim its brilliance and hinder its work in them.

Paul had told the Laodiceans that *"once you were in darkness, but now you are light in the Lord; walk as children of light"* (Ephesians 5:8). Clearly they were not so doing when the Lord wrote to them. What had gone wrong?

Had the pride of the city of Laodicea in its achievements affected the appreciation of the ecclesia that their redemption was entirely of God, by His grace? Had the pride around them in human achievement in material things made it difficult for the brethren and sisters to remember that they had once been dead in trespasses and sins, utterly hopeless and helpless before God? Did they think that God had seen some good in them which was not in others, which led Him to call them? Had they forgotten that God had chosen what is foolish in the world to shame the wise, what is weak in the world to shame the strong, what is low and despised in the world to bring to nothing things that are, so that no human being might boast in His presence? (1 Corinthians 1:27-29).

Had they failed to realise that they could not produce the fruit of the spirit unless the word of Christ dwelt in them richly, that they could only walk as children of the light if they lived continually in the light? We suggest they had forgotten, or ignored, the grace of God that alone had made possible their redemption and the manifestation of the fruit of the spirit in their lives. This attitude of self-sufficiency, of failure to acknowledge their utter dependence on God for all things spiritual, was an abomination to Him, depriving Him of the glory due to Him alone. This is why they were nauseous to Jesus, although they continued to meet as an ecclesia and doubtless observed the outward form of their religion.

Paul's Struggle for the Laodiceans

There is here a lesson for believers today. We may think we shall never make the same mistake as the Laodiceans. Paul told the Colossians how great a struggle he had for them and for the brethren and sisters at Laodicea (Col. 2:1). He went on to write of *"Christ, in whom are hid all the treasures of wisdom and knowledge"* and of believers being *"rooted and built up in him"* (2:3,7). Had Paul detected the beginning of that attitude which the Lord later found so distasteful at Laodicea? How many of the references to grace we have made are taken from the letters to Colossae and Laodicea! And yet they failed to heed Paul's words. We who think we stand must take heed lest we fall (1 Corinthians 10:12). This is especially true of believers who live in the affluent society of the western world.

Alistair Cooke wrote in 1973 in his book *America* that "food in mountainous quantities groans and gurgles from coast to coast (i.e. of the U.S.A.) in variations both succulent and frivolous" (p. 370). He described the luxurious motels provided for the middle class (p. 337) and wrote later of a mounting love of show and luxury. The rest of the western world "scorns American materialism while striving in every big and little way to match it" (p. 387). "Men have landed on the moon, space is being explored and scientists foresee an age-long process of colonisation of the galaxy in which our star is one member" (*The Daily Telegraph*, 7.3.83). There seems no limit to human ambition and achievements.

"I have need of nothing"

This attitude can affect us. Like the Laodiceans, we may forget the grace of God which called us and makes it possible for us to live as His children and replace it by pride in what we regard as our own spiritual achievements. It is still a human trait to echo Nebuchadnezzar's words: *"Is not this great Babylon which I have built by my mighty power . . . for the glory of my majesty?"* (Daniel 4:30). We must not succumb to such feelings, for God still *"resisteth the proud but giveth grace to the humble"* (James 4:6, R.V.; 1 Peter 5:5, R.V. cited from Proverbs 3:34, LXX). *"What have you that you did not receive? If then you received it, why do you boast as if it were not a gift?"* (1 Corinthians 4:7). Jesus humbled himself even to the death of the cross and similar humility must be shown in the lives of believers. The necessity of humility before God and to one another is repeatedly emphasised in the gospels and epistles. There should be among us no pride in what we are, or have, or do. If we lack this humility, we deprive God of what is His alone and we shall be as nauseous to our Lord as were the Laodiceans. Laodicea had a high but erroneous estimate of its spiritual condition. So may we. We may be proud of our spiritual attainments, thanking God that we are not like other men. This attitude is one we must exorcise.

"Not knowing that you are wretched, pitiable, poor, blind and naked." The article is present in the Greek and makes the Lord's words most emphatic. *You* of all others are the wretched one: if there is a wretched, pitiable, poor, blind and naked person, it is you. The

word translated "wretched" occurs elsewhere in the New Testament only in Romans 7:24—*"Wretched man that I am! Who will deliver me from this body of death?"* The preceding verses describe the wretchedness of a man who is carnal, sold under sin, unable to do the things he wanted but doing those he hated. When we appreciate the depth of feeling behind Paul's words we can understand the severity of the Lord's judgement of Laodicea.

The only other occurrence of the Greek word for "pitiable" is in 1 Corinthians 15:19—*"If in this life only we have hope in Christ, we are of all men most pitiable"* (R.V.). If Christ did not rise from the dead, the Christian hope is non-existent and those who trust in him for life everlasting beyond the grave are the most pitiable of men. This is the word the Lord chose to describe the condition of the Laodicean ecclesia.

The Greek word for "poor" is similar to that used of Smyrna in Revelation 2:9, and means abject poverty. It denotes one who has nothing at all. The ecclesia was completely destitute of spiritual riches. The Laodicean ecclesia was "blind" to its true condition. Laodicea was exposed more than most churches to the temptations that came from wealth (cf. 1 Timothy 6:17). Some, perhaps many members, would be wealthy, or at least well provided with this world's goods. Temporal riches may have been regarded almost as a proof that they possessed spiritual wealth also.

"Nakedness" was a symbol of shame and humiliation (e.g. 2 Samuel 10:4-5; Ezekiel 16:36; 23:29; Revelation 3:18 and 16:15). This feeling was so strong that Rome allowed Jews who were to be crucified to wear a loin-covering although criminals were normally nailed to the cross naked.

"Therefore I counsel you to buy from me gold refined by fire, that you may be rich." Notice the gentleness of the Lord's approach: *"I counsel you."* How much harsher the words could have been! Then notice the irony of the advice. An ecclesia of extreme poverty was told to buy from Jesus gold refined by fire, that they may be rich. "From me" and "rich" are both emphatic. It was useless to approach the Laodicean bankers because the Lord alone could give them true wealth.

Again notice the irony. They had been bought by Christ, not with perishable things such as silver and gold but with his own precious blood (1 Corinthians 6:20; 1 Peter 1:18-19; Revelation 5:9, R.V.; 14:4, R.V.). Now they were counselled to buy from him! Those who had nothing could buy the unsearchable riches of Christ without money and without price (cf. Isaiah 55:1-2; Romans 6:23; Ephesians 3:8). Jesus, though he was rich, yet for their sakes became poor, so that by his poverty they might become rich (2 Corinthians 8:9). In Jesus are hid all the treasures of wisdom and knowledge and Paul's prayer for them was that this One may dwell in their hearts by faith, that they might be illed with all the fulness of God. Then they would indeed be rich (Colossians 2:3; 3:16; Ephesians 3:17,19—Note again how many of these references are from the two letters well known to them).

But although these riches could be bought without human wealth, there was a price to pay. The Laodiceans must cease to be self-reliant and self-satisfied. Like Paul, they must count whatsoever gain they had as loss for the sake of Christ; *"count everything as loss because of the surpassing worth of knowing Christ Jesus my Lord ... and be found in him, not having a righteousness of my own ... but that which is through faith in Christ"* (Philippians 3:7-9).

Tested by Fire

The refining of precious metals is repeatedly used as a symbol of the method by which God purges the dross from the character of His people (e.g. Psalm 66:10; Zechariah 13:9; Malachi 3:3). The phrase "gold refined by fire" means gold fresh burned from the smelter. Laodicea had not undergone the refining process and so lacked this gold. One cause was probably their muted testimony to Jesus, which was in such a low key that it did not arouse the antagonism of Jew or Gentile. If they had borne loud and clear witness to Jesus as Messiah and Lord, the coming King of the world, they would inevitably have incurred active opposition. Such witness might cost persecution, and would certainly involve resistance to the spirit of the society in which they lived. Various trials would come on them so that the genuineness of their faith, *"more precious than gold which though perishable is tested by fire"*, might become apparent (1 Peter 1:6-7). Gold refined by fire stands for the spiritual wealth in believers when the dross in their characters has been removed.

"White garments to clothe you and to keep the shame of your nakedness from being seen"—or, better, *"may not be manifested" (phaneroō)*. The Laodiceans were naked in their Lord's eyes but he could clothe them, not with the fine black woollen garments they could buy in the city but with white garments. Just as nakedness was a symbol of shame and humiliation, so clothing with comely apparel imparted honour to the recipient (e.g. Genesis 41:42; Esther 6:7-11; Daniel 5:29; Zechariah 3:3-5; Luke 15:22). When Jesus was transfigured, his garments became intensely dazzling white, as no fuller on earth could bleach them (Mark 9.3; Luke 9:29). The raiment of the angel who rolled back the stone from the tomb of Joseph of Arimathea was white as snow (Matthew 28:3; John 20:12). The elders were clad in white garments as were the armies of heaven (Revelation 4:4; 19:14).

White garments clearly refer to the dazzling purity of the Divine. The Laodiceans had put on Christ—white raiment—at their baptism but they had failed to make this a reality in their lives. They ought to have stripped off the old self with its doings, and have clothed themselves with the new self which is being remoulded into full knowledge so as to become like Him who created it, that is, the Divine. The apostle amplified this. They should have clothed themselves with tenderheartedness, kindness, lowliness of mind, meekness and longsuffering and over all these have put on love (Colossians 3:9-14, Weymouth).

Here is displayed the dazzling purity of the Divine moral life seen in Jesus. Had the Laodiceans displayed these qualities, they would have been clothed in white garments but, lacking them, were naked in their Lord's sight. Unless they abandoned their self-complacent attitude and clothed themselves in these white garments by allowing their Lord's word to dwell in their hearts richly, not only would they continue to be naked before their Lord but the shame of their nakedness would be manifested for all to see (cf. John 2:11; 17:6; 2 Corinthians 4:10,11 etc. for other occurrences of this Greek word *phaneroō*).

THE LETTER TO LAODICEA

"And salve to anoint your eyes, that you may see." Their blindness was not incurable but it was useless to go to the physicians of the city for their eye salve because this could not cure the type of blindness from which the ecclesia was suffering. The Lord, the Great Physician, alone could supply the eye salve that would restore their spiritual sight, just as he had given sight to the blind man by anointing his eyes with clay (John 9). *"The eye is the lamp of the body. So, if your eye is sound, your whole body will be full of light; but if your eye is not sound, your whole body will be full of darkness. If then the light in you is darkness, how great is the darkness"* (Matthew 6:22-23; cf. Luke 11:34). Once, the eyes of their hearts had been enlightened but there was always the risk that they would again *"live as the Gentiles do . . . darkened in their understanding, alienated from the life of God"*. They had not so learned Christ and the apostle repeats his exhortation of Colossians 3:9-14 which we quoted above (Ephesians 1:18; 4:17 and on). *"The commandment of the Lord is pure, enlightening the heart"* (Psalm 19:8).

We can see ourselves as we really are in God's sight only by using the eye salve of His word. Self-knowledge is one of the most difficult qualities to acquire; it was essential to their life in Christ and was obtainable only if they looked at themselves through the spectacles of his word. Notice particularly that nothing that society could offer, gold, fine black garments or eye salve, could meet their extreme need. Each must buy for himself from the Lord; purchase for others was not possible (Matthew 25:9-10).

"Those whom I love." The "I" is emphatic. Had the Lord not loved them, he could not have written this letter. Love was consistent with a true appraisal of their condition. The Lord spoke unpalatable truths in love. The Lord's words are reminiscent of Proverbs 3:11-12—*"Whom the Lord loves he rebukes (reproves)."* In the LXX the verb "love" is *agapaō* and this is retained by the writer to the Hebrews when he cites Proverbs (Hebrews 12:5-6), but the Lord here used *phileō* instead of *agapaō*. *Phileō* is a word more charged with emotion than *agapaō*. The change was made deliberately to remind those whom he had sharply rebuked that they were nevertheless dear to him. It was a token of friendship

THE LETTERS TO THE SEVEN CHURCHES OF ASIA

to the ecclesia which, of all the seven, least deserved it. Here was the Great Shepherd searching for the sheep who had strayed (Matthew 18:12).

"I reprove and chasten." Again the "I" is emphatic. There are no exceptions to this rule. *"The Lord disciplines him whom he loves, and chastises every son whom he receives"* (Hebrews 12:6). The word translated "reprove" means to expose (e.g. John 3:20; Ephesians 5:11,13). The sin is exposed to bring the person concerned to acknowledge his fault (Trench, *Synonyms*, p. 13). David, reproved by Nathan, confessed his sin and was forgiven, but he could not escape chastisement. The child born to him and Bathsheba would die and the sword would never depart from his house (2 Samuel 12:7-14). Acknowledgement of sin is an essential precursor of the chastisement by which the child of God is trained and so reproof and chastisement were evidence not of Christ's rejection of the Laodiceans but of his love, of the depth of his feeling for them.

"Be zealous and repent." The word translated "zealous" occurs nowhere else in the New Testament. It means "be hot", a condition absent from the ecclesia (vv. 15-16). It was difficult to boil over with enthusiasm for the Gospel in an atmosphere like that in the city, but the tense indicates that the Lord required this as a permanent element in their characters whereas "repent" refers to a once-for-all act, the firstfruits of "be zealous".

"I stand at the door and knock." There are many allusions to other parts of Scripture in these words. A person knocking at a door spoke to identify himself (e.g. Acts 12:13-14). Disciples were bidden to be on the alert so that they could open to their Master at once when he knocked (e.g. Luke 12:36) but here the tense of the verb "knock" indicates continued knocking to give the Laodiceans the opportunity to respond. They would be familiar with travellers and traders arriving after the city gates had been closed for the night and knocking repeatedly to obtain entry; but it depended on those within the city whether the gates were opened. The Lord's appeal is now to individual members of the ecclesia: *"If any man hear my voice."* They had in effect excluded him from their lives and now they were asked to let him in, to allow his

THE LETTER TO LAODICEA

word, his commands, his example increasingly to control their lives. But they had to act; the Lord would not knock indefinitely or force an entry (cf. Luke 24:29).

The whole passage is reminiscent of the Song of Solomon. First, the words of the bride: *"I slept but my heart was awake. Hark! my beloved is knocking."* Then the words of her beloved: *"Open to me, my sister, my love, my dove, my perfect one."* The response of the bride: *"I had put off my garment, how could I put it on? I had bathed my feet, how could I soil them?"* Between sleeping and waking she had been slow to open the door and when at length she did so *"my beloved had turned and gone"* (Song 5:2-6). There is a warning here to the Laodiceans and all believers. Undue delay in opening the door to the Lord would mean that he had gone when they finally did so.

"I will come in to him and eat (literally "sup", R.V.) *with him and he with me."* Supper was then the main meal of the day when work was over; it was a leisurely meal, participation in which was a token of affection and at which there was an opportunity for long and intimate talks. Thus the word, or its related noun, is used of the supper at which the memorial service was instituted (John 13:2,4; 21:20; 1 Corinthians 11:25), of this memorial service (11:20) and for the marriage supper of the Lamb (Revelation 19:9). But notice that they would sup with him as well as he with them. Each had to contribute. The Lord was offering a mutual fellowship between himself and those who responded to his invitation. He would not pay a fleeting visit but make his home, his permanent abode, with them (cf. John 14:23; 17:20-23). What amazing grace the Lord showed to an ecclesia to which he could give no word of commendation!

The same Lord seeks entrance into our lives but we alone can admit him. The Laodicean brethren and sisters maintained the routine of their meetings, otherwise they could not have thought themselves spiritually rich; but they were so self-satisfied that they did not feel the need for the transforming power of Christ. It is difficult for those who are comfortably provided with this world's goods to give the Lord and his work absolute priority in their lives, to be zealous, boiling in his service.

THE LETTERS TO THE SEVEN CHURCHES OF ASIA

Here is a lesson for modern disciples in the Western world who live in a society in which enthusiasm in divine things is unfashionable. We can maintain the routine of our services while all too easily settling into a condition of spiritual self-satisfaction, taking our responsibilities lightly and enjoying the pleasures available today. We may say that we have the Truth, that we are therefore rich, but this may not be apparent in our lives. We must honour in our manner of life the commitments made at baptism, showing in a competitive society the meek and quiet spirit which is the hallmark of a true believer. To be the elect of God is not to be His pampered favourites but to be challenged to a loyalty, service and sacrifice that know no limits. God's chosen people recognise that any service they render, any sacrifice they make are wholly inadequate responses to the riches of the grace given them.

The Judge is at the Door

There are activities in this life we cannot escape but we must take great care that our lives are not swamped by them. The Laodiceans had Paul's letter to them and to the Colossians but they failed to profit by them. We have the whole Word of God in our hands but this will not help us unless we allow its teaching increasingly to control our lives. The day when our Lord will return and knock is near. We of all generations of believers can say that the Judge is standing at the door. The night has far gone, the day is at hand. Let us examine ourselves as honestly as we can through the Word, because if we have tended to exclude the Lord from our lives, the time for repentance and opening our lives to him may be short.

10

TO HIM WHO CONQUERS

BELIEVERS have been called to God's eternal glory. Their bodies will be fashioned anew that they may be conformed to the body of Jesus' glory (Philippians 3:21, R.V.) and they will reign with him (2 Timothy 2:12). The apostles tell us little more than this about the life the conqueror will then enjoy. It is true that Paul wrote: *"What no eye has seen, nor ear heard, nor the heart of man conceived, what God has prepared for those who love him, God has revealed to us through the Spirit. For the Spirit searches everything, even the depths of God"* (1 Corinthians 2:9,10). But he later adds that *"our knowledge is imperfect . . . for now we see in a mirror dimly, but then face to face. Now I know in part, but then I shall understand fully"* (13:9,12).

In addition to the inability of the finite mind to comprehend the infinite, human language—even when used by inspired apostles—is inadequate for the full expression of the glories of everlasting life. Even the beloved apostle, closest of all to the Lord, experienced this: *"Beloved, we are God's children now; it does not yet appear what we shall be, but we know that when he appears we shall be like him, for we shall see him as he is"* (1 John 3:2). It is as if John had written that he could not fully describe the life to come; he could only tell them one thing that was all-embracing and all-sufficient. They would become like the risen glorified Lord but the difficulty of detailing in human language what this meant remained.

About the time John was writing his epistle, the Lord himself put into words as much as the human mind can understand of the life to be given to those who conquer. This was done to encourage his brethren and sisters to be faithful to him even at the cost of their lives. These promises combine to give a composite picture of the glory to be given to those who overcome, expressed in a series of wonderful figures. There is a progression in these. The duration and quality of the life to come are first described and then figures are used to show how those who conquer will become the Lord's intimate friends, exercising his authority over the nations and, the ultimate promise of all, sharing his throne.

We live in troublous times which, as we saw when considering the letter to Smyrna, will become increasingly difficult as the day of the Lord draws nearer. May we, like those early disciples, be encouraged by these promises to be faithful whatever the cost, so that we may by God's grace share in them.

EPHESUS

"To him who conquers I will grant to eat of the tree of life which is in the paradise of God." The Greek word *nikaō* is translated "overcomes" as well as "conquers". The word occurs far more frequently in John's writings than in the rest of the New Testament. The Ephesians would be reminded of the Lord's words they must have heard from John: *"Be of good cheer, I have overcome the world"* (John 16:33). There is a ring of victory in John's use of this word in his first epistle and in the Revelation (e.g. 1 John 4:4; 5:4,5; Revelation 12:11; 15:2). The believer can overcome as his Lord conquered. The promise is couched in emphatic terms. The Greek, literally translated, is *"to him who overcomes, to him ... "*. "To him" is repeated for emphasis. The promise is immutable.

"Paradise" is a Persian word which found its way into both Greek and Hebrew and means a park or pleasure ground. It is so used in the LXX especially of the garden in Eden which the Lord planted (Genesis 2:8 etc.; Numbers 24:6; 2 Chronicles 33:20; Nehemiah 2:8; Ecclesiastes 2:5; Song of Solomon 4:13). Adam, after his sin, was barred from the tree of life *"lest he put forth his hand and take also of the tree of life, and eat, and live for ever—therefore the* L ORD *God sent him forth from the garden of Eden"* (Genesis 3:22-23). Adam therefore did not live for ever but returned to the dust from which he had been made. God, having expelled Adam, placed east of the garden of Eden cherubim *"and a flaming sword which turned every way, to guard the way to the tree of life"* (Genesis 3:24, R.S.V. and

TO HIM WHO CONQUERS

Young's *Literal Translation*). The words imply that the way to the tree of life would not be barred for ever but was guarded until access could again be granted. The conqueror will be given such access and, eating of the tree of life, will live for ever.

The foundation of future glory is thus the bestowal of immortality, the promise that the victors' lives will be lived in bodies free from every human disability. *"They are now before the throne of God, serving him day and night in his temple and he who is seated on the throne shall overshadow them with his care"* (Moffatt); *"spread his tabernacle over them"* (R.V.); *"shelter them with his presence"* (R.S.V.) (Revelation 7:15). What a lovely promise! God will overshadow those who conquer with His care and there will therefore be no more worries, anxieties or cares to oppress them. *"Never again will they be hungry, never again athirst, never shall the sun strike them nor any scorching heat; for the Lamb in the midst of the throne will be their shepherd, guiding them to fountains of living water; and God shall wipe away every tear from their eyes"* (Revelation 7:16-17, Moffatt).

Blessings beyond Description

We cannot now visualise a life that knows no end but when this is associated with freedom from every human disability we are attempting to use human language to express ideas for which it is inadequate. It will help if we think of Jesus. He was subject to disabilities similar to those experienced by his followers. The Lord suffered hunger, pain, fatigue and death. The apostles were his companions in that life and then, for 40 days, they saw him alive, freed for ever from all such disabilities. He had become a being in whom dwelt all the fulness of the Godhead bodily (Colossians 2:9), who was the *"effulgence of his (God's) glory and the very image of his substance"* (Heb. 1:3, R.V.). The Lord fully reflected the glory of God which even Moses could only see in part. The apostles saw a perfect immortal body.

Some of the statements made about the Lord's resurrection body are so startling that we find it difficult to grasp them. He could enter a room when the doors were closed, move at will from place to place and rise against the force of gravity. The Lord led the disciples to Bethany, seen by them but presumably invisible to the Jews. We can only accept that the resurrection body in which God's physical glory was seen in its fulness was wonderful beyond our understanding or ability to express in words but we can be certain that we shall be utterly content if we awake in his likeness. The promise that the victors would eat of the tree of life was peculiarly appropriate to Ephesus. The ecclesia hated the works of the Nicolaitans and among other things its members therefore would not eat foods offered in sacrifice to idols. Such abstinence would be rewarded by granting them access to the tree of life. The Nicolaitans took the fruit of the pagan world in which they lived and this led to death; the victors would eat of the tree of life and live. Believers of every age are thus reminded that abstinence from the passions of the flesh, from every form of evil in this life, is a necessary precursor to eating of the tree of life (1 Peter 2:11; 1 Thessalonians 5:22).

There is yet more to be learned from the Lord's words. The first Adam had grasped prematurely at equality with God and was consequently expelled from Eden. The last Adam, subjected to the same temptation, *"did not count equality with God a thing to be grasped, but emptied himself, taking the form of a servant, being born in the likeness of men. And being found in human form he humbled himself and became obedient unto death, even death on a cross"* (Philippians 2:6-8). As a consequence, he was able in the mercy of God to open the guarded way to the tree of life but the victors were reminded of the cost of this re-opening. Two words are used in the New Testament and LXX for tree. *Dendron* is used of the living tree; *xulon* refers primarily to wood cut and ready for use, to anything made from wood, a stick, a cudgel or a pole, gibbet or cross (for which the word *stauros* is usually used in the New Testament). *Xulon* can also be used of a living tree. The Acts of the Apostles and the Epistles use *xulon* to denote the tree on which the Lord was hanged (Acts 5:30; 10:39; 13:29; 1 Peter 2:24; cf. Galatians 3:13) and this word is used five times in the Revelation of the tree of life. The inseparable connection between the tree on which the Lord was hanged and the tree which will give immortal life is thus emphasised and the victors are reminded of the price of their redemption. (It is interesting to speculate why the LXX translators used *xulon* in the early chapters of Genesis to denote the tree of life.)

SMYRNA

"Be faithful unto death and I will give you the crown of life . . . He who conquers shall not be hurt by the second death." Do not fear those who can only destroy the body but remain faithful to me, even at the cost of your life, and I will give you the crown of life. Note the contrast: be faithful *unto death* and I will give you the crown *of life*. The Greek has an article and the promise literally translated reads, "I will give you the crown of the life"; that is, I will give you the life as your crown.

The Greek word *stephanos*, translated "crown", is used of:
(a) the laurel wreath worn by the Caesars;
(b) the crown given to the victors in the games;
(c) the garland worn by a worshipper while engaged in the service of a pagan deity. This garland was sacred to the particular god. Thus myrtle was worn for Aphrodite, ivy for Dionysus and wild olive for Zeus Olympias.

In the New Testament, *stephanos* usually refers to the emblem of victory in the Olympic games (1 Corinthians 9:25; 2 Timothy 4:8; 1 Peter 5:4; cf. 2 Timothy 2:5) (cf. "The Letter to Philadelphia", p. 103).

The figure would be easily understood by the brethren and sisters in Smyrna because the city was famous for its games. It was especially appropriate to an ecclesia facing a contest with the devil and would be understood as the garland of victory if they overcame.*

The garland of victory was "The Life". *"That which was from the beginning, that which we have heard, that which we have seen with our*

---

* In the accounts of the trials of Jesus, the Gospel writers refer to the crown (*stephanos*) of thorns placed on the Lord's head (Matthew 27:29; Mark 15:17; John 19:2). This was part of the blasphemous masquerade of royalty the Roman soldiers inflicted on Jesus. Tiberius wore a laurel wreath. This man is said to be a King; let us give him his *stephanos* but make it thorns rather than laurel. And let us clothe him in purple like the emperor and give him a reed as his sceptre!

eyes, that which we beheld, and our hands handled, concerning the Word of life (and the life was manifested, and we have seen, and bear witness, and declare unto you the life, the eternal life, which was with the Father, and was manifested unto us)" (1 John 1:1-2, R.V.).

Perfect Life in a Perfect Body

We saw under the promise to Ephesus that the risen Lord fully manifested the Divine physical glory which Moses could only see in part. There was also a divine moral glory in the revelation to Moses consisting of mercy, grace, goodness and truth (Exodus 34:6-7). The words of those who later spoke from God reiterated and amplified the declaration to Moses but words cannot convey the full meaning of these qualities. This could only be done by showing them in a human life. And so *"the Word became flesh and dwelt among us, full of grace and truth; we have beheld his glory, glory as of the only Son from the Father"* (John 1:14). The Lord manifested God's name, God's perfections, the qualities associated with the name proclaimed to Moses, to the men God gave him out of the world: *"I have shown the men whom you took out of the world and gave to me what you are really like"* (John 17:6, Barclay). The Lord is the image, the visible and exact representation of God's moral character. In him, God's moral attributes of mercy, grace, goodness and truth were perfectly displayed in a life lived under the conditions of ordinary human existence. He was radiant with the Divine glory and bore the very stamp of God's nature (2 Corinthians 4:4; Colossians 1:15; Hebrews 1:3).

This was "the life", the eternal life which was with the Father and which John says they saw manifested in Jesus. This is the garland of victory promised to those who are faithful to death. The reward is not just life in a perfect body but perfect life in a perfect body. There will then be complete and perfect fellowship between the Father, the Son and the conquerors, thus fulfilling the Lord's high-priestly prayer (John 17:21)

The emblem of victory was not a perishable garland like that given to the victors in the games, but imperishable, an unfading crown of glory (1 Corinthians 9:25; 1 Peter 5:4). Those who receive such a crown cannot be "hurt by the second death", a phrase occurring only in the Revelation and used of the final end of the rejected from which there can be no release. The promise is emphatic in the Greek: the one who overcomes will by no means be hurt by the second death.

There may also be in the promise an allusion to the garland worn in the service of pagan gods. The brethren and sisters at Smyrna who did not enter idols' temples and who thus refrained from service to such deities would nonetheless be given a garland, an infinitely more precious one, to wear when they served the Lord perfectly in the kingdom, a garland of The Life.

The concept of complete fellowship between the Father, the Son and the victors is amplified in later promises.

PERGAMUM

"To him who conquers I will give some of the hidden manna, and I will give him a white stone, with a new name written on the stone which no one knows except him who receives it." We have seen that the sin of this ecclesia was similar to that of the Israelites in the wilderness who were seduced by Balaam and so this part of the promise was couched in terms which recalled the wilderness. The manna eaten in the wilderness was normally corruptible but some was preserved throughout their generations in a golden urn placed, hidden, in the ark of the covenant (Exodus 16:32-34; Hebrews 9:4). Corruptible manna was made incorruptible by the power of the Spirit of God, in the Most Holy Place and thus became a symbol of incorruptible spirit life. One is inevitably reminded of the comparison between the manna which sustained this life only and the bread of life which came down from heaven and would make immortal those who partook of it (John 6:30-58).

Notice again how appropriate this promise was to those at Pergamum who did not follow the teaching of Balaam and therefore did not participate in feasts in pagan temples. They would be given food of infinitely greater value, the hidden manna. The Lord's ascension hid him from human sight but not for ever. In due time, the hidden manna will be brought forth from the Holy of Holies so that the conquerors may eat of it. Their life is now hidden with Christ in God, but when Christ, who is their life appears, they will appear with him in glory, will be made like him for they will see him as he is.

Although, as we have seen, Pergamum was famous for the parchment made in the city, this perishable material was not suited to bear the name to be given to those who were now incorruptible. The new name was therefore inscribed on a white stone. This was a *tessera*, a small block of stone, ivory or similar substance, with words or symbols engraved on one or more faces. Tesserae with distinctive marks were used by a host inviting friends to a banquet in an idol's temple to ensure that uninvited persons were not admitted.* The tesserae the Lord promised will admit the conquerors not to pagan feasts but to the marriage supper of the Lamb.

The most remarkable of these stones were the *tesserae hospitales*, given to indicate that a contract of friendship, the so-called covenant of bread, had been made between two persons. This was ratified by an exchange of tokens, usually tablets inscribed with the names of the contracting parties or some engraved device. Sometimes only one tessera was used and divided into two parts so that the two halves could be fitted together, thus preventing the forging of a tessera and the making of a false claim on friendship. Since the tesserae were exchanged, none could know the name or device engraven on it but the donors. These tesserae were preserved as family heirlooms and a descendant of one of the parties to the contract had only to present his token long after the original contract was made, to a descendant of the other party, for his claim to be honoured. The tesserae the Lord will give are "white", the word used of the transfigured Lord (Matthew 17:2; Mark 9:3; Luke 9:29), of the glorified Lord (Revelation 1:14) and of angelic raiments (Matthew 28:3; John 20:12; Acts 1:10; cf. Daniel 7:9; Revelation 19:14). The Lord's tesserae will not approximate to white as might those made from marble but will be dazzling white as the Lord was at his transfiguration. The symbol denotes absolute purity and perfection.

---

*Specimens of such tesserae giving the bearer admission, for example, to the temple of Dionysus at Athens are in the British Museum.

TO HIM WHO CONQUERS

On each tessera a new name will be written. The names we have today merely serve to identify us but in Biblical times a name described the character of the person named; it told what he was. Thus when the LORD proclaimed His name, he enumerated the qualities that made up His character. New names were given in Scripture to show that the persons concerned had or would become changed persons. Thus Abram became Abraham, Sarai's name was changed to Sarah, Jacob's to Israel and Simon's to Peter (cf. Isaiah 62:2; 65:15). Two Greek words are translated "new" in the New Testament, *kainos* and *neos*. The latter word denotes the "new" primarily in reference to time and does not occur in Revelation. *Kainos* is used primarily in reference to quality, that which as recently made is superior to what it succeeds. It is used in Revelation of the Lord's new name, the new Jerusalem, the new song and of all things made new (3:12; 5:9; 14:3; 21:1,2,5). The new name written on the stone thus signifies that the recipient of the tessera is a changed person, having a perfected character which is far superior to that which it replaces.

These figures show that the conquerors will be admitted to intimate friendship with Jesus, that there will be the closest possible communion between them and their Lord. The Gospels show the greatness of the Lord's friendship with the disciples but words cannot express the full depth of meaning of his friendship given to the conquerors in the age to come. We can perhaps best say that Paul's words will then be fully realised: the old will have passed away and the new come; we shall be a new creation in Christ (2 Corinthians 5:17).

THYATIRA

"He who conquers and who keeps my works unto the end, I will give him power over the nations, and he shall rule them with a rod of iron, as when earthen pots are broken in pieces, even as I myself have received power from my Father; and I will give him the morning star." The Lord in these letters repeatedly refers to his knowledge of the works of the brethren and sisters but this is the only occasion when an ecclesia is exhorted to keep his works to the end. There is here an allusion to verse 22: *"Behold, I do cast her (Jezebel) into a bed, and them that commit*

adultery with her into great tribulation, except they repent of her works" (R.V.). On the one hand are the works of Jezebel to be repented of, and on the other the Lord's works, those he did, to be kept to the end. Notice the emphasis on the need for perseverance "to the end".

The word translated "power" is *exousia*, not the more widely used *dunamis*. *Exousia* is more than mere power. A moral quality is often implied so that it means power exercised responsibly (e.g. John 1:12; 5:27; 17:2). The authority promised the conquerors will be exercised in accordance with divine principles. It is the might of right and not the right of might.

The promise of the Father to His Son was, *"Ask of me, and I will make the nations your heritage, and the ends of the earth your possession. You shall break them with a rod of iron, and dash them in pieces like a potter's vessel"* (Psalm 2:8-9). As has been seen, the only occurrence of the phrase "the Son of God" in Revelation is in the opening verse of the letter to Thyatira. One reason for the use of this title has already been discussed but it also seems as if the Lord wished to draw attention to it before alluding to Psalm 2. The power, the authority, was not the Lord's inherently, but given to him by his Father as a reward for overcoming. The tempter offered the Lord all the kingdoms of this world on his terms but the Lord refused. The brethren and sisters at Thyatira were tempted to conform to pagan customs for fear of hardship but those who refused would be given authority over the nations.

The authority received by the Son from his Father will be shared by him with those who conquer. Here is one consequence of the friendship between the Lord and the conquerors promised in the previous letter. The greatness of the gift emphasises the depth of friendship between the Lord and the victors.

The Greek word translated "rule" (*poimainō*) means to act as a shepherd (Psalm 2:9, LXX footnote; cf. Marshall's interlinear translation of Revelation 2:27; cf. John 21:16; Acts 20:28; 1 Corinthians 9:7; 1 Peter 5:2; Revelation 7:17). The eastern shepherd carried a rod, usually hung from his girdle. The rod (*rhabdos*, the word the Lord used and which appears in Psalm 2:9, LXX and

22(23):4, LXX) was a strong wooden club about two feet long which often had a large number of heavy iron nails driven into its rounded head, rendering it a deadly weapon in the hands of a shepherd against wild animals or men. The conquerors will, with Jesus, shepherd the nations with a rod of iron (cf. Revelation 19:15), exercising authority responsibly but breaking them in pieces if they are wilfully recalcitrant. Only thus can the kingdoms of this world become the Kingdom of our Lord and of his Christ (cf. Daniel 2 where "clay" is rendered "earthenware" in the LXX; also Isaiah 30:14; Jeremiah 19:11). This done, the Lord and the conquerors will shepherd those that are left of the nations and bring them to God. (It is interesting to note that *rhabdos* is twice translated "sceptre", in Hebrews 1:8, where the righteousness of the Lord's *rhabdos* is emphasised.)*

The only other occurrence of the words translated "morning star" is in Revelation 22:16, where Jesus said: *"I am the root and offspring of David, the bright morning star."* The morning star is Christ himself, and the Lord will give them himself, identify himself completely with them, and with that will come every spiritual blessing. This is a reiteration of the promise of divine life to the conquerors, of their admission to the closest possible friendship with their Lord.

SARDIS

"Yet you have still a few names in Sardis, people who have not soiled their garments; and they shall walk with me in white, for they are worthy. He who conquers shall be clad thus in white garments, and I will not blot his name out of the book of life; I will confess his name before my Father and before his angels." We have seen that the garments of the

---

*The Hebrew of Psalm 2:7 means "You shall break them with a rod of iron", whereas the Greek is "tend as a shepherd". The difference is more apparent than real since, as we have seen, both concepts appear in the Lord's words. The original Hebrew text was made up of consonants only and vowel points were not added until long after Psalm 2 was written. Scholars say that the consonants in the Hebrew underlying the English versions and that from which the LXX was translated are identical and differ only in the vowels read with them. The Lord did not here endorse the LXX as against the Hebrew but used the dual meaning which could be drawn from the consonanted text.

majority at Sardis were soiled when they allowed the spirit of ease, self-indulgence and lethargy in the society in which they lived to affect their lives in the Truth. Those who had not so done would walk with the Lord in white. As we saw under Pergamum, white was the symbol of absolute purity and perfection (e.g. Matthew 17:2; 28:3; Revelation 7:9; 19:11). How appropriate this promise was to those who had not soiled their garments! He who conquers shall be clad *thus* in white garments: thus, in the manner just described, by not soiling his garments. Note the words "with me": here is another indication of the closeness of those who conquer to their Lord.

"And I will not blot his name out of the book of life." The negative is emphatic as in the promise to Smyrna—I will by no means, in no wise, blot out his name (cf. John 6:35; 8:51). There are references in the Old Testament to a book kept by God (e.g. Isaiah 4:3; Daniel 12:1; Malachi 3:16). One is inevitably reminded of Moses' plea for Israel's sin: *"But now, if thou wilt forgive their sin—and if not, blot me, I pray thee, out of thy book which thou hast written."* But the LORD said to Moses, *"Whosoever hath sinned against me, him will I blot out of my book"* (Exodus 32:32-33).

The concept is developed in the New Testament where the book is associated with life (Philippians 4:3; Revelation 17:8; 20:12,15). This book of life is now in the hands of the Lamb and so it is called the Lamb's book of life (Revelation 13:8; 21:27). The Lord has power to add names to this book or to delete them; hence the promise, *"I will not blot his name out"*. Believers' names are entered into this book at baptism; erasure of a name will result in condemnation when the Lord returns in judgement. Again, how appropriate this promise was to Sardis. The names of those not sunk in the torpor of spiritual death will remain in the Lamb's book of life, and they will be among those who will live for ever.*

---

*There may here be an allusion to the custom that famous cities then kept a register of their citizens or others who had the right to participate in the privileges and advantages conferred by that city. A name was erased at death ("you are dead") or for some grave misdemeanour when the person concerned lost the right to these privileges.

TO HIM WHO CONQUERS

"I will confess his name before my Father and before his angels." The Lord here combines Matthew 10:32 and Luke 12:8 to include both the Father and His angels. The context of these passages and of Luke 9:26 clearly indicates that the Lord is referring to the judgement when he returns in glory. Those who conquer will then be acknowledged, accepted, by the Lord. Again, notice the Lord's concern for Sardis. The letter to such an ecclesia closed on a note of encouragement.

PHILADELPHIA

"He who conquers, I will make him a pillar in the temple of my God; never shall he go out of it, and I will write upon him the name of my God, and the name of the city of my God, the new Jerusalem which comes down from my God out of heaven, and my own new name." Note the fourfold repetition of "my God" for emphasis. The word translated "pillar" (*stylos*) occurs twice only in the New Testament outside the Revelation: *"James and Cephas and John, who were reputed to be pillars"* (Galatians 2:9); *"the household of God, which is the church of the living God, the pillar and bulwark of the truth"* (1 Timothy 3:15). The concept of the pillar is clearly that of a support, the apostles to the household of God and this in turn to the truth. The temple of God to which the Lord refers is a building of people: *"You are fellow citizens with the saints and members of the household of God, built upon the foundation of the apostles and prophets, Jesus Christ himself being the chief cornerstone, in whom the whole structure is joined together and grows into a holy temple in the Lord; in whom you also are built into it, for a dwelling place of God in the Spirit"* (Ephesians 2:19-20; cf. 1 Peter 2:3-7; 1 Corinthians 3:16-17; 2 Corinthians 6:16).

Those at Philadelphia who conquered, who had in this life been joined together with the chief cornerstone, with all that implies, will become pillars in God's perfected dwelling place. What a delightful promise to an ecclesia which had but little power! They would become supports in God's temple. There may here be an allusion to Isaiah 22 from which the Lord had quoted earlier in this letter. There may also be a reference to the custom that a man who had served the city or state well had, as his memorial, a pillar erected in one of the temples with his name inscribed on it.

THE LETTERS TO THE SEVEN CHURCHES OF ASIA

Moreover, there is no contradiction between the promise to Philadelphia and Revelation 21:22. There is no separate temple in the holy city because each of its constituents is now God's dwelling place. The temple of Revelation 3 is now, so to speak, incorporated in the city and so no longer has a separate existence.

The apostles, although pillars, did not abide; they went out in death. Those who are pillars in this temple will never "go out". They cannot be removed while the building stands. As with the same words in the promise to Sardis, the Greek is emphatic: *by no means* will they go forth any longer. Like the Son, they will continue in the house for ever (John 8:35). As we have mentioned earlier, the city was so subject to earthquakes that at one time many of the inhabitants lived outside it in tents. In God's temple there would be no need to go outside for safety. They would dwell in the house of the Lord for ever (Psalm 23:6). How apposite this promise was to Philadelphia, and its wealth of meaning would be appreciated by them (cf. Isaiah 56:5). Was this promise a reminder that, although they were troubled by the synagogue of Satan, who falsely claimed to be Jews, the promise of God through a Jewish prophet would be fulfilled in them?

"I will write upon him the name of my God, and the name of the city of my God, the new Jerusalem which comes down from my God out of heaven, and my own new name." Compare Revelation 7:3; 9:4; 14:1; 22:3-4; also the plate of gold worn on Aaron's forehead (Exodus 28:36-38). Mention has already been made under Smyrna and Pergamum that the name of God stands for His character and it is unnecessary to enlarge on this.

The name of the LORD was put upon the people of Israel; they were called by His name (Numbers 6:27; 2 Chronicles 7:14; Jeremiah 14:9; cf. Isaiah 63:19). Those who were called by the name of the LORD were to show in their lives the moral characteristics of that name (Jeremiah 13:11; Malachi 2:2). By and large, Israel failed in this duty and so time and again is accused of profaning and polluting God's holy name. They did not manifest in their own lives the character of the LORD revealed to them (Jeremiah 34:15-16; Ezekiel 36:20; Malachi 1:6,12).

TO HIM WHO CONQUERS

Only here and there were there those who did so and then only imperfectly. This was true also of the brethren and sisters at Philadelphia because of the weakness of human nature, but the conquerors were promised that the character of God will be written on them so that their characters will then be divine (cf. Smyrna). The days of imperfection will have gone for ever.

In addition to the existing natural city of Jerusalem there is another Jerusalem which is above, the heavenly Jerusalem (Galatians 4:26; Hebrews 12:22). The Philadelphians acknowledged that here they had no continuing city but sought the city to come, whose builder and maker is God (Hebrews 13:14; 11:10). Their citizenship was *"in heaven; from whence also we wait for a Saviour, the Lord Jesus Christ"* (Philippians 3:20, R.V.). The culmination of their hopes would be when the holy city, the New Jerusalem, came down out of heaven from God (Revelation 21:10). Roman citizenship was the highest honour Rome could confer but citizenship of the New Jerusalem is incomparably greater. The citizens of the New Jerusalem will be those on whom the Lord writes the name of the city of his God; they will have the right to enter the city by the gates (22:14).

The Lord's new name may be a title to be given him at his coming, a symbol of his full glory then to be revealed. If this is so, the meaning of this new name written on believers would be that the full glory of being God's children will be revealed to them when the Lord returns (cf. 1 John 3:2; Colossians 3:4). There may also be a reference to the tessera with a new name, discussed under Pergamum.* Alternatively, the new name may be a title given to Jesus only in the Revelation, in which case the obvious choice would be "The Lamb". The word translated "Lamb", *arnion*, means literally "little lamb" and is used 29 times of Jesus in the Revelation. It occurs elsewhere only in John 21:15 where it is not used of the Lord. This name expressed Jesus' humiliation and glory, his sacrifice and exaltation. This name written on the

---

* A new name may be a reference to the city which had twice been renamed, first Neocaesarea as an appreciation of Tiberius' help in rebuilding the city after the earthquake in A.D. 17 and later Flavia, in honour of the family name of Vespasian.

conquerors would remind them that the glory of everlasting day had been won for them by a slain lamb. Whatever the Lord's new name is, those upon whom it is written will be utterly content.

LAODICEA

"He who conquers, I will grant him to sit with me on my throne, as I myself conquered and sat down with my Father on his throne." What a wonderful promise to make to members of an ecclesia in which the Lord could find nothing to praise! Jesus had already promised the apostles that *"when the Son of man shall sit on his glorious throne, you who have followed me will also sit on twelve thrones judging the twelve tribes of Israel"* (Matthew 19:28; cf. Luke 22:29).

An even greater promise is here made: the conqueror will sit with Christ on his glorious throne. The Greek has "in" (*en*) my throne, not "on" (*epi*). Matthew 19:28, already cited, has *"on his glorious throne"* (cf. Matthew 25:31; Acts 2:30; Revelation 4:2,9; 5:1,7,13; 6:16). The Lord's use of "in" is surely significant. The conqueror will not be seated on a separate throne but permitted to share his Lord's throne. Eastern thrones were then much broader than today (more like a sofa, as one commentator put it) and there was room on it for others than the one who occupied it by right. A seat on the right hand of the occupant of the throne was the position of greatest honour, and the next highest privilege was to be seated on the left (1 Kings 2:19; Psalm 110:1; Matthew 20:21; Mark 10:37; Ephesians 1:20; Colossians 3:1; Hebrews 1:13).

The Lord had been permitted to sit with his Father in God's throne because he had conquered. The conqueror will be enthroned with his Lord as Jesus was enthroned with his Father. The Master will share the fruits of his victory with the conqueror even to the sharing of his throne. Again, there cannot be a stronger intimation of the closeness, the fulness of the fellowship between the Lord and those who conquer, reflecting the oneness of Jesus and the Father Himself. Jesus' likening it to him sitting in his Father's throne shows that he could offer them no greater honour.

The Laodiceans had the hardest battle to fight of any of the ecclesias if they were to overcome and so appropriately the greatest reward is promised to them. The Lord had had the most difficult battle of all to fight but he had succeeded and so could they if they heeded what Jesus had said to them. There could be no greater incentive to reform and overcome than this promise.

Epilogue

Let us summarise as briefly as possible the lessons modern believers can draw from the experiences of these early ecclesias.

An ecclesia may toil unremittingly in the Lord's service, do its utmost to guard the deposit entrusted to it and yet fail. Zeal in seeking out and exposing error can easily degenerate into a censorious hypercritical spirit which leads to heresy hunting. Error must be exposed but not in such a way that love is lost and with this the distinguishing badge of a true ecclesia. The Truth must be preserved but in love, with the gentleness of Christ. Without these, all our other qualities are as nothing.

An ecclesia of abject poverty, subjected to severe tribulation and defamation, had not grumbled about its lot, had not been provoked against its persecutors, but had allowed love to control its actions and words. The brethren and sisters could have escaped persecution and poverty by offering a pinch of incense on Caesar's altar and calling him lord, but they rejected this easy way of escape. We expect a period of intense trouble before our Lord returns. We do not know what trials await us but the ecclesia at Smyrna has left us an example of how to face them and win our Lord's approval.

Love must not be confused with weakness. Members of an ecclesia may wish to enjoy the pleasures of society around them even if this puts them in situations which compromise the manner of life they ought to live. The requirements of employment may lure them into similar situations. Lack of separation from the attractions of life around them is as dangerous as heresy hunting. Right conduct is as important as purity of doctrine. Believers must not compromise with society in such a way as to jeopardise their witness to the Christian life.

An ecclesia may appear to other meetings to be flourishing but in reality be asleep. None of its works is brought to completion;

THE LETTERS TO THE SEVEN CHURCHES OF ASIA

they are only half performed. The danger is that such an ecclesia may be satisfied with itself and unconscious of its true condition. Each ecclesia must examine itself in the light of the Lord's assessment of Sardis and avoid failing as did their brethren and sisters there.

Faithful witness and preaching is possible even if an ecclesia has only a little power. Such can keep their Lord's word and not deny his name.

An ecclesia may be well content with its spiritual condition, feeling it is rich, prosperous, in need of nothing and unaware that in reality it is wretched and pitiable. When an ecclesia feels it is prosperous spiritually, then is the time for it to examine itself through the Lord's message to Laodicea.

These letters were for the brotherhood at large and not only for the seven ecclesias to which they were sent. Similarly, the promises contained in them combine to form a picture of the glory to be revealed in the age to come. Every ecclesia, each individual, will in this life be subjected to difficulties and dangers. The promises are for each one who conquers and keeps his Lord's works to the end. May our Father richly bless us and bring us to the glories of His Kingdom.

"He who has an ear, let him hear what the spirit says to the churches."